FAT WON'T MAKE YOU FAT
" Not All By Itself "

The truth about the
foods you eat, from

L. Lee Coyne Ph.D.

FISH CREEK PUBLISHING
Calgary, Alberta Canada

Address inquiries to the publisher:
Fish Creek Publishing
240-70 Shawville Blvd.S.W., #76084
Calgary, AB, T2Y 2Z9 Canada

Canadian Cataloguing in Publication Data
Coyne, L.Lee, 1939 -
Fat Won't Make You Fat : "Not All By Itself"
Includes bibliographical references and index
ISBN 0-9682609-0-X

1. Reducing diets. 2. Nutrition. 3. Health. I. Title.
RM222.2.C69 1998   613.2'5   C98-910460-5

Cover design by *Matt M. Moche* of Calgary
Printed and bound in Canada by *Calgary Colourpress*

DEDICATION

I dedicate this book to my first Granddaughter Saidy who was born while I was writing this book. I sincerely wish that her paradigms will be flexible so she may adapt to this rapidly changing world. May she grow to be as special as her parents, my son Geret and my daughter-in-law Carol.

TABLE OF CONTENTS

Preface 1

1 Introductory Stuff 5

2 A Paradigm Shift 9

3 Science or Science ? 17

4 Historical Stuff 27

5 Technical Stuff 45

6 Insulin - Good Guy / Bad Guy ! 61

7 Protein is the Answer 71

8 Let's Eat !! 85

9 The Stuff you are not Eating 119

10 Get Physical 139

11 More Good Stuff 149

Resources 166

Bibliography 167

Notice

This book is not a substitute for the advice of a licensed
health practioner. Discuss medical problems, disorders and
illnesses with your health practioner.

PREFACE

STUFF YOU SHOULD READ IMMEDIATELY

PLEASE do not take the information in this book as a license to over indulge in any one nutrient. Over-eating any of the macro nutrients (carbohydrate, fat or protein) will make you fat. Understand that this book does not promote a high fat diet. This book promotes an understanding of a balanced diet but the new balance will require you to make a paradigm shift. It should help you get out of the "Calorie & fat gram counting syndrome" which has not worked over the century.

This book came about through a sequence of events.

First was a little of my personal experience with what kinds of foods helped or hindered my own weight management and health over the years.

> **This book does not promote a high fat diet!!**

Second was the release of several (some would say too many) books, some old, but several in the last 6 years which caught my attention. They all promote the common thread of "lower Carbohydrate and higher protein" food selection. The degree of carbohydrate restriction varies from very low to moderate. The major disagreements seem to be the fat intake recommendations The major point of agreement is that too much insulin production from too much carbohydrate consumption is the major problem with weight management and other common health related problems.

Third was the publication of some recent sports nutrition research involving insulin production after exercise and the role it plays in energy recovery and muscle building.

This little link brought the whole picture into focus for me. Consequently, I decided to share my explanation of this puzzle.

This book is about much more than weight loss. It is about health. It is a condensation of the concepts outlined in the books I referred to. It is a Book about Books. These books are listed in the reference section if you feel you need to read more.

Most of the chapters will stand alone in terms of explaining particular concepts. So if you are not science or technical in orientation, you may skip the "Technical Stuff" section and still benefit from the explanations.

When you review the concepts presented, please do not fall into the Calorie counting "arithmetic" trap. Too many critics of this concept are "hung up" on the standard methods of assessing dietary advice and have not tried anything new.

Do not fall into the Calorie counting "arithmetic trap" These critics usually assess any dietary plan, which may be different from the standard, by judging it on the same arithmetic as the standard was created. This cannot be done because the calorie recommendations assume a certain macro-nutrient combination. It is well understood that if a diet is higher in high quality protein, the food consumption will be reduced. It should also be understood that there is no nutrient recommendation for grams of carbohydrates like there is for protein or essential fats so do not be too quick to judge. **Just try it!!**

If you have not tried this new balance, then please do not criticize it until you have. Remember that these concepts are based on research that goes back over a century and a half. There is a new body of research blossoming around the world that supports the concepts delivered.

As we go to press, a news item appeared, reporting from the International Congress of Nutrition held in Montreal in late July of 1997, with the following headline **"Pass the fat, hold the pasta"**. Naturally it is sensationalized a bit for good press, but it is a report on a paper presented by Dr. Walter Willett, chairman of the nutrition department at Harvard School of Public Health. Dr. Willett indicated **there is considerable evidence** that the over-simplified low fat, high-carbohydrate diet is making people fat. Enette Larson and associates from the University of Alabama, published a paper in 1996 in the *American Journal of Clinical Nutrition* which showed that dietary fat on its own plays a minor role in increasing body

Pass the fat, hold the pasta!!

fat. In fact their research found that just 2 percent of the weight gained by 135 men and 214 women could be attributed solely to dietary fat. This is further evidence to be added to that discussed throughout this book indicating a change in dietary guidelines seems to be in order because the current system does not seem to be working.

It's time for a shift of paradigms away from the **"low fat / high carbohydrate modest protein diet"** to the time tested **"higher protein / modest fat/ lower carbohydrate"** program. Read on and give it a try.

1

INTRODUCTORY STUFF

Any writer would be disappointed if the reaction to his/her book was "Oh No, not another diet book". If that is your reaction, I understand completely because I have the same response several times every year. Just when you believe you have seen the last "I have all the answers to why people are fat" books and programs, another twist is offered. Frequently the "twist" may be just that-- a re-hash of old concepts wrapped in

> **OH NO!**
> **NOT ANOTHER DIET BOOK!**

new packaging or jargon. Well, this book has a little of that, but I hope you find it a bit refreshing and of some value.

Several issues prompted me to write this book. In no particular order these issues include:

1. Over the last seven to eight years there has been a plethora of books on this particular subject or phase of nutritional advice. Most of which are 300 or more pages long, filled with tantalizing success testimonials and seemingly complicated recipes and menus, all included to encourage you to try the particular plan. This is not a critique of such books but rather a realization that many busy people are discouraged from taking the time to read such dissertations. The reasons vary from apparent time constraints to fear that the programs are too complicated and will require too many calculations and too much record keeping. I believed there was a need for a book of short duration which "Cut to the Chase" so to speak. This book reviews the science and the

procedures behind other consistent programs and offers a condensed version of the concepts. **So this is a book about books.**

2. It seems to have become obvious that the high carbohydrate - low fat diets are not working. North Americans eat less fat and more carbohydrate than ever before and yet there is an obesity epidemic which has health-care professionals both puzzled and worried. One does not need formal statistics on fat reduction in the diet to confirm that we eat less fat. Just read a few popular magazines with their "low-fat" or fat cutting advice columns or visit your local grocery store and count the "low-fat" or "fat-free" products available. Of course you understand that in the free enterprise world products which do not

The second epidemic is that of Type II Diabetes

sell do not last in the market place very long. Obviously these products are selling and are therefore part of the North American diet.

3. A second epidemic is that of Type II Diabetes. Based on the annual incidence of new Diabetics published in Canadian Diabetic Association information brochures, we discover a new Diabetic every eight and one half minutes (8.5 min) in Canada. I recall five years ago when discussing this at one of my public lectures, the figure was one every twenty-three minutes (23 min.). That is a dramatic 3 fold increase in a very short time.

4. Research for this book helped me to explain why there are some over weight vegetarians and why a vegetarian diet (currently , very politically correct in some circles) is not suitable for everyone. Think about it. If fat makes you fat ,

there should not be any overweight vegetarians.

The information and concepts in this book are not new. They have been reviewed and promoted as early as the year 1825 in an essay published by Jean-Anthlene Brillat-Savarin entitled "Preventative or Curative Treatment of Obesity". I

> **Concepts described in this book are not new!!**

quote from that essay "Now, an anti-fat diet is based on the commonest and most active cause of obesity, since, as it has already been clearly shown, it is only because of grains and starches that fatty congestion can occur, as much in a man as in the animals;....that a more or less rigid abstinence from everything that is obviously starchy or floury will lead to the lessening of weight."

To carry this one step further, and answer the question - how do you "fatten" a pig or a cow? - **You feed them grain, not fat!**

Later I will outline the "Historical Stuff" regarding the concepts in this book. After reading it I am sure you will scratch your head and wonder about some of the popular scientific so-called wisdom which currently promotes the high carbohydrate - low fat - low protein- low calorie diets of today.

2

A PARADIGM SHIFT

The Concept

The concept of this book is one of a review of current knowledge, some old and some recent, primarily from a series of books which have become popular. I guess you could say that I have "bought into" or am promoting, because of science, logic and experience, this "Better Balanced Diet" concept

It has become apparent that to achieve and maintain optimal health (which is much more than mere absence from disease) and optimal weight management or control, North Americans need to make some changes. Primarily they need to increase their protein intake, decrease their carbohydrate

A Diet is the food you eat, regardless of why you chose it!!

intake (particularly from grains and refined sources), consume adequate essential fatty acids, regularly engage in some form of moderate fat burning -- muscle building physical activity and follow a responsible food supplement program.

"The word diet needs clarification. Everyone is on a Diet. Diet is the food you choose to live by. Nutrition is what you receive from the food. Ignore people who suggest that their program is not a diet but 'a new way of eating'. That just means that the diet you choose is different. There are weight loss diets, athletes diets, high energy diets etc. Diet is not a synonym for weight loss"

Now I know this program or review is not part of the

conventional wisdom, standard recommendations world we all grew up to respect. No matter what field of endeavor you pursue, you will find that standard practices will produce standard results. If you want exceptional results, you must exercise exceptional practices. This applies to the arts, sports, business success and even love. Today, standard results in the health care world (which is really a disease care world- but that would be another book) in relation to nutrition are such dismal statistics as forty-four per cent of hospital beds are occupied bye people who did not eat enough protein. Eight out of ten of the top risk factors in coronary heart disease are dietary related. In spite of all the fat reduction dietary programs promoted in the last 45 years, The American Heart Association announced in early 1996 that for the first time since 1980, deaths from cardiovascular disease are increasing. Standard recommendations do not seem to be working.

> **Standard practices will produce standard results**

When you see the reference list at the back of this book and appreciate that each of those books are based on 100 to 400 references (Sears Enter the Zone book is accompanied by thirty-eight pages of peer-review references), you will realize that I am not alone in my thoughts and interpretations. The reasons for the apparent misguided route recommended by government health agencies, and health care professional and academics are numerous. Some deal with poor or incomplete science followed by the exercise of jumping to conclusions. Some reasons are political in motivation and some are economic, while others may merely be misinterpretation of good existing scientific data and experience. Scientists and health care professionals are not immune to observing rigid paradigms even when they are outdated. The paradigms in which we operate will always affect our interpretations.

Remember that Dr. William Harvey in the early 1600's was ill regarded for his description of the human circulation as a closed system. His ideas were originally regarded as not consistent with the current wisdom of the day. There was also Louis Pasteur who was considered a medical heretic for suggesting that "germs" caused disease and that surgeons should practice sterilizing their environments.

Eggs and butter became the bad guys!!

Even today there is the Cholesterol and the egg issue. Some 45 years ago when an apparent correlation between blood cholesterol levels and heart disease was reported, the egg and butter industries became the bad guys. Because both foods were high sources of cholesterol, recommendations spewed forward for a restriction in their use in the name of reducing the risk of heart disease. Today, with half the dairy cooler in your local grocery store filled with a non dairy product - margarine and a continuing campaign against the egg, we find that heart disease is on the increase. Incidentally, the research used to damn the egg employed animals, and dehydrated egg yolk powder and according to Dr. Atkins and Louise-Ann Gittleman, was financially supported by the Cereal Institute of America. Since that time, it has been learned that eggs, upon reassessment, have less cholesterol than originally reported and apparently the cholesterol content is dependant upon what the chickens eat. Several other reports indicate the method of cooking the egg affects the cholesterol action. Apparently soft cooked yolks remaining whole, as in soft poached or boiled, cause fewer problems than overcooked hard boiled, scrambled or fried eggs. A recent newspaper head line was "Go ahead, have an egg". The article was reporting on a study from the University of Washington, presented at an American Heart

> **"Go ahead have an egg"!!**

Association meeting in October of 1995. Eating an egg raises cholesterol only slightly, if at all, for most people". Research has not been able to confirm that cholesterol consumption is the cause of elevated blood cholesterol. Even Dr. Ancel Keys, who first published the predictive equations for dietary fat effects on blood lipids and heart disease, was recently quoted in "Eating Light" magazine to say **"...there's no connection whatsoever between cholesterol in food and cholesterol in the blood. None. And we've known that all along."** Yet in spite of current data, you will have difficulty accepting the idea that liberal egg consumption is acceptable. Particularly if you were educated in the other paradigm. Even the common man is reluctant to change paradigms.

So you see that science and particularly medical or health science does not usually move forward quickly nor are its interpretations always correct. There are many controversies yet to be solved including healthy weight management along with understanding and achieving healthy nutrition.

Back to the concept of this Book

Many dietary trends have surfaced in North America that need to be addressed if we wish to improve the health of the population in general. Once again, without putting specific complicated numbers to the concept, the majority need to:

> a) increase their protein intake. Eat protein in every meal and every snack

    b) decrease their carbohydrate intake (Particularly from grains & refined or processed sources)

    c) ensure the consumption of adequate good fats for energy and essential fatty acids for metabolism

    d) eat more often, but smaller meals of course.

    e) consume a responsible food supplement program to ensure a complete diet.

and   f) exercise regularly at moderate intensity to build or maintain energy burning muscle and metabolize fat.

Please understand, that in general, low calorie, low fat - high carbohydrate diets have not been

> **Eat protein in every meal and every snack!!**

working and there is very good science to explain why. Also understand that the two quickest ways to decrease your rate of metabolism (your ability to burn Calories) and consequently gain weight or not lose weight are a) don't t eat and b) don't exercise.

    So you may identify with this concept and to signify that this program contains some differences, I have dubbed it **"The Better Balanced Diet"** or **BBD.** Remember, I did not promise new and revolutionary knowledge. I promise a review and interpretation of old and new scientific information blended into an easy to follow program. This program has lots of similarities to others discussed throughout the book. What I propose, is most like the " Zone" program of Dr. Barry Sears. There are several modifications and hopefully some simplifications. There is nothing particularly wrong with "The Zone" program but I feel it is a little conservative on protein recommendations, supplementation, fiber and may be a little more rigid with the fats than I feel necessary. I have offered a simplified entry into the 40 - 30 -

30 diet concept. (In case you haven't caught on to the jargon, the conventional diet is approximately 55% Carbohydrate, 30% Fat and 15% Protein some refer to it as the 55 - 30 - 15 diet and the recommendations for athletes is a 60 - 20 - 20 diet by many "authorities"). You will also find items in this program which are consistent with Gittleman of " Beyond Pritikin", The Eades of "Protein Power", Maffetone, author of "In Fitness and in Health" and the Hellers from "Healthy for Life".

Now that you have the concept, you may if you wish go directly to the food selection chapter and begin the program. You should read the chapter on ' Insulin, Good Guy / Bad Guy ', to help you understand why you are selecting some of the food combinations. If you are of an academic enquiring mind you will, I think, enjoy reading the remainder of the book.

There is no ideal diet suited for the entire species!!

The Balanced Diet

There is no ideal diet suited for the entire species Homo Sapiens (mankind). One diet fits all is a shibboleth of lazy dietary advisors. Dietary needs are determined by genetics and environmental factors. A discussion of this topic would require another book. Each individual must explore the range of nutrient requirements to meet their needs. Once a level of health is reached efforts should be toward continuing with the diet which created such a condition. This means feeling and functioning at some optimal level, including clear headed, disease free, energy in surplus, recovering from exertion easily , sleeping well, etc.. If you are not operating in this "Zone" (to use the title and concept of Dr. Barry Sears) you need to change in order to get into the optimum zone.

Long ago it may not have been so difficult because most people tended to be born, live and die within a relatively small geographical area. Consequently the "survival of the

So, what is a balanced diet??

fittest" phenomena prevailed and those with the correct genetic make-up survived utilizing the nutrients available in that geography. Hence the Inuit thrives on a much different diet than Polynesians, or Northern European or the native of South Africa. Today, with population mobility and available food mobility, combined with growing genetic diversity in the human race we face new problems. Only the individual can listen to their bodies and know for sure what that feeling of well being means.

So what is a "balanced diet" and who set up the rules for this balance? How were the rules determined? Basically the so-called "balanced diet" or the Pyramid (Rainbow in Canada) guidelines were established by a committee of "experts" and endorsed by various government agencies and health associations. It has been based on epidemiological data and some questionable assumptions like cholesterol consumption determines blood cholesterol. In a single statement, the Standard North American Diet (SNAD) has not been working very well. It is time to make a shift, closer to what nature determined or provided and that is what the BBD is all about.

The "Standard North American Diet has not been working very well!!

3

SCIENCE OR SCIENCE ?

My objective for this chapter is to help you become critical, objective and analytical in matters of nutritional advice. This position paper about research in the nutrition industry, if you are experienced in such matters, will be somewhat elementary and simplistic. However, for most people, I am concerned that some "blind faith" in government and expert advice has lead North Americans down a health path that is less than successful. Hopefully this introduction to research methodology will move you past the "blind faith" stage into an analytical and logical stage. You will understand that there is science and then there is good science - hence the name of this chapter.   "Blind Faith" seems to be the reason for our love a f f a i r   w i t h carbohydrates, fear of

> **"Blind faith" seems to be the reason for our love affair with carbohydrates !!**

fat and indifference toward or aversion to protein and the trace nutrients (as demonstrated by the reluctance of experts to recommend food supplements). To achieve optimum health, these attitudes must change.

A Lesson in Research Methodology

Logic and experience make significant contributions to science, particularly when interpreting scientifically collected data. You see, it is logic and experience which can give meaning to data or even help to design sound experimental procedures. I felt a need to write this brief chapter because I believe that all too often data can be translated into fact by the media or by well-meaning writers without a due process review of the logic and experience

> **The shift to a 40 - 30 - 30 diet will not seem illogical !!**

component. If the interpretation is flawed and has become part of the current paradigm then a paradigm shift becomes more difficult. Possibly after you read the following, you may be more willing to examine your paradigms and the shift to a 40-30-30 diet will not seem illogical.

Research can be divided into three major categories:
- a) experimental, usually involving cell cultures or animals with the occasional human trials.
- b) clinical, which, by nature of its name, means intervention on human subjects.
- and c) epidemiological, which is large population studies which may be acute (todays data) or longitudinal (data over time). The longitudinal studies may or may not involve intervention.

Experimental research, usually in cell cultures or on laboratory animals, is often the first step in hypothesis testing. However it remains only the first step because animals may and do have very different hormonal and enzyme control mechanisms from humans. There are always similarities, because we usually use small mammals and man is a mammal. Cell cultures, on the other hand, are another story. There is a significant difference between keeping a few cell or tissue samples alive for observation in a petri dish in a very controlled environment with very controlled nutrient samples and the complex act of preparing food in the kitchen, eating it and digesting it in hopes that the nutrients contained will eventually arrive at the appropriate cell. The latter is a very complicated stream and is known as human nutrition.

Epidemiological research involves selecting a large population with certain criteria like geography, nationality, professional background, health history, age, gender, etc. and measuring a number of parameters on the entire population. These parameters would then be followed at intervals over a period of time and various correlations and or patterns, if any, would be studied. There has been an explosion of research papers, based on epidemiological projects, appearing in the literature in recent years. Papers based on data collected from the Framingham Mass. study, which lasted for 30 years, the Tecomseh Michigan study, the Caerphilly Wales Heart Disease study, the Helsinki Heart Study, the Paris Prospective study, The Lipid Research Clinics Coronary Primary Prevention Trials, the Physicians' Health Study , the Health Professionals study , the Nurses' Health study, and many more. Each of the foregoing listed studies has generated many published papers.

Once again, the results from correlation data published must be considered preliminary in the absence of experimental and clinical trials. Correlation does not guarantee causation but epidemiological studies do

Correlation does not guarantee causation!!

provide both cross-sectional and longitudinal data from which experimental and clinical studies may emanate. Until these studies appear the advice to the consumer will remain 'caveat emptor'. Certain assumptions are made, during the study design phase, which establish the protocol and data collected. Often ignorance of other influencing factors (ignorance implies lack of knowledge, not intentional distortion of data collection) may exclude it / them from the collection process and therefore from the interpretation process. I refer to one example of this in the next chapter when Dr. Ancel

Interpret epidemiological studies with a very critical eye !!

Keys reported on the alleged correlation of saturated fat consumption, blood cholesterol and heart disease. Data collected emphasized fat & cholesterol consumption and totally ignored carbohydrate consumption. This should be considered a serious oversight in view of today's knowledge of the role of refined carbohydrates on insulin production and the resulting hormonal and cardiovascular implications.

So, interpret epidemiological studies with a very critical eye before buying into some of the reported implications reported or interpreted by an overzealous press.

More About Research Methods

Nutrition scientists over the last fifty years have attempted to become very scientific and observe all the rules of using conventional experimental models, protocol and statistics. Experimental groups and control groups are carefully selected for double blind designs conducted in controlled environments using controlled nutrients and establishing a controlled baseline. Unfortunately some of the conventional protocols do not serve nutrition research very well.

A double blind study usually means that you
a) select a defined group (population) with certain characteristics to study. Ideally, if the population is very large, you might randomly select a "sample" from the larger

population. Often the sample size is based on availability of resources, i.e. laboratory space or procedures or cost of each procedure - all those practical things.

b) The sample to be studied is then divided into at least 2 groups, one of which is a "control group" who do not receive any alteration in their diet or lifestyle. Sometimes they administer a "placebo" which is something that looks like what the experimental group (the other group in the study) is receiving but effectively should have no affect. This little exercise is an attempt to control the potential psychological effects. Sometimes people can be convinced of benefits or detriments in advance and that can affect, for short periods at least, the results. The other half of the group, known as the experimental group, receive the experimental protocol. Sometimes the groups are selected at random but in other designs they might be paired with a control group member with similar characteristics i.e. age, gender, health conditions, weight, fitness scores etc.

> **Sometimes people can be convinced of benefits or detriments**

c) "Double Blind" means the principle investigator, just like the participants (subjects), does not know to which group each subject has been assigned. This is to prevent the investigator from tampering, consciously or unconsciously with the subjects or their data. The subjects do not know which group they are in or that there are groups. Hence the phrase "Double Blind".

d) Following a predetermined time period (hopefully based on some scientific rationale and not the University calendar of a soon to graduate research student needing course credits on time) the data are summarized and statistically analyzed. Based on these finding and statements of "statistical significance" the investigators draw summaries and conclusions. If there is a difference in results between the groups, the statistical significance procedures used will signify that the results are significant at the .05, .01, .001 or some other level of confidence. These numbers are a statement of the degree

The relevance of this review will now become evident !!

of certainty that the results, if the experiment were repeated, would be the same in 99 out 100 times for .01 or 95 out of 100 times for the .05 level. To allow a scientific finding to become fact, the controlled experiment should be repeated numerous times to be sure this wasn't the one in one hundred occasion that produced the result. Then the experimental results must stand up to clinical experience in the real world to become an absolute fact.

The relevance of this little review of the "scientific method will now be made evident.

The design described works very well when one studies the effects of administering certain drugs or the introduction of foreign substances into an environment where there is very little chance of interfering interactions from the subjects. Drugs, for instance, are usually such small molecules that they easily enter the body without interference. There are no existing saturation levels and usually the body doesn't produce the item or obtain it from other sources. Consequently the typical "controlled" experimental model, just explained, works very well in assessing the effectiveness of drugs. However, when it comes to altering nutrients, the story changes. No nutrient exists, survives, or functions by itself in nature. Nutrients normally come from complex food sources, and their concentrations and availability are affected by food quality, the health of the digestive system, genetics of the hormonal system and the general health of the recipient. Consequently, to alter the consumption level of a single nutrient without regard for all the other

> **Nutrients normally come from complex food sources**

factors involved in the normal retrieval and metabolism of this nutrient, may be a fallacious exercise. Quite a different exercise from that of administering a specified dose of penicillin or some other drug.

An example might be the alteration of the intake of the mineral calcium by adding to a diet some quantity of calcium in the form of tablet supplements. To ensure a good experimental design, one should also proportionately alter the intake of magnesium, phosphorous, vitamins B-1, B-2, D and possibly protein to truly study the affects of added calcium. Care should be taken that the calcium supplement is digestible (some are not) and free of toxic substances like lead or mercury (which some do contain).

The "fat & cholesterol is bad for heart disease" may serve as another example of apparently good science, by a reputable scientist, gone bad. About 50 years ago, Dr. Ancel Keys, (wrote a book "Biology of Human Starvation") the guru of many modern nutritionists, published work which demonstrated that populations with varying degrees of heart disease showed a strong correlation with fat intake and later with blood cholesterol levels. Interestingly though, at the same time in England, Dr. John Yudkin (who wrote the book "Sweet and Dangerous") was reporting near identical correlations between incidence of heart disease and sugar or refined carbohydrate intake. The reality was that most of the culture studied showed strong correlations between fat intake and sugar intake. Even of more interest was the fact that Keys studies and most American studies dealing with fat and cholesterol consumption in connection

Yudkin wrote the book "Sweet and Dangerous"

with heart disease, did not even bother to record carbohydrate consumption. There was apparently a built in paradigm which assumed that sugar and carbohydrates couldn't have anything to do with heart disease because the apparent etiology of heart disease involved blood vessel occlusions with fatty substances. Other examples, difficult to explain with the North American paradigm of heart disease and fat are:

a) In Iceland, heat disease was almost unheard of until the 1930's even though their diet is very high in fat. However, in the early 1920's refined carbohydrates and sugar were introduced. Twenty years later, Iceland struggles with heart disease just like the rest of the "civilized world".

b)The former Yugoslavia and the country of Poland developed heart disease in the late 1940's and early 1950's and it coincided with the quadrupling of sugar intake and occurred despite a fall in animal fat consumption.

c) The famous Framingham Mass. study seemed to support the paradigm of the day by showing a correlation between blood cholesterol levels and the incidence of coronary heart disease. However they could not show a correlation between fat consumption nor cholesterol consumption and the rate of heart disease. Science now tells us that through excess insulin production, brought on by excess refined carbohydrate consumption, coupled with low essential fat intake, is responsible for the excess low density (bad) cholesterol production and not fat or cholesterol intake.

The latter is a glaring example of an epidemiological study misinterpreted. Correlation does not mean does not mean causation. Correlation studies should lead to other studies and must be defined with logic, experience, experimental research , clinical research and other scientific rationale. Epidemiological studies are not experimental studies. They are "large population over a period of time" reviews.

It should also become apparent that studying a single nutrient or nutrient to disease relationship leaves you with one very important question...what else were they eating? or ...what were they not eating? ... or what was their current state of health

It's What You Don't Eat that Counts !!

and nutrition? In my lecture (and book in progress) entitled "It's What You Don't Eat That Counts" I review this concept in detail. It means that the interrelationship of current health status to **all** the required nutrients, which operate in concert with each other, determines ones health. It is not the surplus or deficiency of a single nutrient that determines your physiological response but rather the entire package of nutrients, genetics, and environment. If one exhibits certain symptoms, they may respond to the consumption of higher or lower levels of selected nutrients or groups of nutrients which would be considered a therapy. Once the therapy has corrected the problem, the goal should be to maintain a complete diet (some would call it a balanced diet) suitable for the individual to maintain good or optimal health.

So my point here is -- don't try to correct all health problems by altering just one or two factors. ---rather look to optimize your health by managing the whole package of variables which contribute to excellent health. (Namely complete nutrition, exercise, stress reduction, environmental management, etc.)

Some would call it a balanced diet !!

4

HISTORICAL STUFF

History should help us learn. There are two parts to this historical stuff. One is my personal experience which lead to this book and the second is simply a review of significant published contributions to the concept of the **"Better Balanced Diet" (BBD).**

Personal Historical Stuff

I knew in my early years as a University student that if I "cooled it" with the sugars, breads, potatoes and starchy foods, I controlled my weight easier. Shortly after leaving high school I started to struggle with my weight. (I have never been obese but at 5' 5", I have reached 185 pounds, in spite of reasonable physical activity as a University athlete and later as a recreational athlete.) This weight management problem coincided with being fully employed and being well paid, working in the oil patch in Western Canada. In other words, I

The restricting of carbohydrates was discouraged !!

could now afford to buy and did buy and eat lots of food that I really liked. Nutritional quality had not yet entered my vocabulary. However as I became more "educated" the restricting of carbohydrates was discouraged in favor of reducing fat and protein foods which were the"standard" recommendations handed down by the Health & Welfare Canada offices and the Dietetic Associations. So, wanting to fit into traditional academic excellence, I followed, to a degree, standard recommendations - most of the time.

In the late 60's after my Doctoral studies, I started teaching exercise physiology at University. Then I started reading every-thing I could about nutrition because many of my students and some private fitness consultation clients were asking questions which required intelligent answers. My personal weight progressed back and forth between 170 pounds and 185 pounds. I knew that if I "cooled-it" with my carbohydrate consumption (particularly beer, wine, bread, cereal and sugar) that I managed my weight with greater ease. However, this meant I tended to eat more protein foods, particularly eggs and beef. This pattern was not considered orthodox nor balanced in my

You may have experienced the same patterns !!

academic circles. Consequently I struggled for many years with this dilemma and I suspect that if you are reading this book that you may have experienced the same patterns.

Published Historical Stuff

Weight loss had just begun to become a major growth industry in the 60's and early 70's. The Weight Watchers concept took on a new and competitive look. **The "Stillman Diet", the" Dr. Atkins Diet Revolution" and "The Scarsdale Diet"** were the big three among best selling diet books. All three programs advocated by these three clinicians were carbohydrate restricted diets and two of these books are still very popular. (could it be because they work?) They were all criticized because they were known as **Ketogenic diets** (explained in the 'Technical Stuff' chapter) and feared to be dangerous. We now know that dietary induced ketosis (excreting of ketone bodies), which may cause temporary body and breath odor for awhile, is not in fact dangerous.

I "played" with the Atkins Diet and found it actually did work but was always discouraged by colleagues with allegations of the unhealthy nature of such diets. As an aside, I find it interesting that in 1992 Dr. Atkins revised and republished this material in **"The Dr. Atkins New Diet Revolution"** - a full 20 years after the first book. I also have since learned that the late **Dr. Carlton Fredericks** (I have been one of his fans for years) published his **CFLC Diet** in 1965. The CFLC (Carlton Fredericks Low Carbohydrate Diet) advocated carbohydrate be

> **Carlton Fredericks was not the first to promote carbohydrate restriction !!**

restricted to 60 grams per day which is a little more gentle than the Atkins 20 grams per day. One dinner roll or 1 apple is 20 grams of carbohydrate.

However, Carlton Fredericks was not even the first to expound upon the benefits of restricting carbohydrates for weight management and health reasons. Several authors have re-published the famous **"Letter on Corpulence" by William Banting, first published in 1864**. Banting (not to be confused with Frederick Banting, co-discoverer of Insulin in 1921 at the University of Toronto) reviewed his personal history of excess weight (corpulence- this word is old but is still in your dictionary) along with various health problems and the lack of success of conventional therapies. However, using a carbohydrate restricted diet, he experienced success. He was five feet and five inches (5' 5") in height and weighed in excess of 200 pounds. (I can relate to his height but not that much weight) Over a period of carbohydrate restriction he lost fifty (50) pounds and maintained the new weight throughout his remaining years. He died at the age of eighty-one (81) years. In fact, during those years, dieting for weight loss became popularized as "banting". If you were on a weight loss diet you were considered to be banting.

Apparently, in the late 1800's the physician attending the Earl of Salisbury rediscovered the Banting letter and successfully treated the Earl, using the low carbohydrate-high protein -moderate fat regime. This was the introduction of the "Salisbury Steak"- a term for chopped

> ## The Earl of Salisbury re-discovered the Banting Letter !!

(ground) meat cooked like a steak- and the menus used were published under the name **"The Mahda Diet"** in a book, published by a New York magazine, entitled **"Eat and Grow Thin"**. A book which was very successful and went through 112 printings by 1931.

In the late 1920's the first "scientist" joined the list of investigations regarding the effectiveness and wisdom of restricting carbohydrates. **Vilhyalmur Stepfansson and Karsten Anderson,** two Arctic explorers, reported that Eskimos lived well on a **meat-only diet** and successfully completed intense work tasks involving considerable energy expenditure. Both explorers volunteered to be studied in Bellevue Hospital in New York City for twelve months. Their diet was approximately 2500 Calories per day and seventy-five (75%) per cent of those Calories came from fat. In one year they both lost six (6) pounds and their blood chemistry including cholesterol was considered to be normal. No adversity was reported as a result of consuming this unorthodox diet.

During the late 1950's and early !960" **Dr. John Yudkin** published work on the restricted carbohydrate diet rationale and its corresponding success. His books **"The Slimming Business"** and **"A-Z of Slimming"** were very popular. He also published a paper in Lancet (a British Medical Journal) entitled **"The Treatment of Obesity by the 'High Fat' Diet. The inevitability of Calories"**. His most famous book is likely **"Sweet and Dangerous"** published in 1972.

These last two references to carbohydrate reduction for weight loss were conducted by members of the respected academic community and not mere laymen reporting on personal experience nor clinicians attempting to fill their clinic with overweight patients.

Not clinicians attempting to fill their clinics !!

I personally left the "low carbohydrate" concept alone through the late 1970' and 1980's but I did develop a serious interest in the health-giving benefits of protein. I review, actually I "hammer" the concepts pretty hard, the virtues of protein in my lecture and soon to be released book **"Protein is the Answer"**.

More Recent History

In 1990 I read a book **"The Endocrine Control Diet"** by **Calvin Ezrin** which was the first thorough explanation I had read of why lower carbohydrate and higher protein diets work. None of the previous authors in the popular books wrote with clarity about the underlying science behind carbohydrate restriction as an effective means to weight loss and health improvement. The Ezrin diet is a 'softer' Atkins type of diet. Where Atkins begins with only 20 grams of carbohydrate, Ezrin begins with 40 grams. But even more impressive was the fact that Ezrin is a professor of Endocrinology at UCLA and had received his graduate education under Doctor Best of

> **Atkins begins with 20 grams**
> **Eades' begins with 30 grams**
> **Ezrin begins with 40 grams**
> **Fredericks began with 60 grams**

the Banting and Best combination, the two University of Toronto Endocrinologist s who discovered insulin. So, not only was I reading the first academic to describe the mechanisms for the nemesis of insulin but a very credible academic at that. Most of the previous popular writers were essentially successful clinicians. Ezrin's book opened my eyes to the problems that excesses of the very necessary hormone could create and helped me realize that many people needed a "different" balanced diet.

I find it interesting that Ezrin's book never seemed to "catch fire" in the marketplace like it should have. Maybe the title was too scientific to become part of modern culture. I wonder if a new catchy title might not have sold more books? Just a thought regarding how knowledge is transmitted.

My next excursion was into the **"Carbohydrates Addicts Diet"**, a book by the husband -wife team of **Rachael and Richard Heller** who are both researchers and professors at Mt. Sinai School of Medicine in New York and at the Graduate Center of the City University of New York. Once again, two academics outlined a program which explained the excess insulin connection. I originally picked up this book on a lark after a friend wanted me to offer a scientific critique of the material presented. I must admit, at first, I thought the program was a hoax (my paradigm had not yet made a complete shift). However, some coinciding events helped to change my paradigm.

Their diet plan, in simplest words, involved two consecutive meals with virtually no or very little carbohydrate, followed by the third meal (known as a 'reward' meal)

a program which explained the excess insulin connection !!

consisting of anything you wanted as long as you consumed it in less than one hour. These rules received lots of chuckles from me and my friends. The chuckles change to one of those **"A - Ha' s!"** when I read some research conducted by Dr. John Ivy's laboratory at the University of Texas and published in the Journal of Applied Physiology in 1992. The project was to evaluate recovery sport drinks and it was sponsored by The Shaklee Corporation and lead to the development of a new recovery product called 'Physique'.

Using 33 athletic subjects who rode stationary bicycles in a two hour race intensity simulated ride, they studied the insulin response to 3 different recovery drinks. When the heavy exercise was completed, blood insulin levels were almost non existent. The subjects then consumed one of three drink mixtures. Drink A) was 40.5 grams of protein, drink B) was 112.5 grams of carbohydrate and drink C) contained both. These quantities and ratios were previously established through other published studies. They did not just arbitrarily decide on them, there was good science involved in the decisions about the drink combinations tested.

Drinks were consumed immediately after exercise and again 2 hours later. Drink A) - protein, produced a modest rise in blood insulin, drink B) provided a significant rise and drink C) produced the largest insulin response. The real significance of this study toward understanding the concept in this book is that the first drink - immediately after exercise cessation - produced a sharp rise in insulin which peaked at about the one hour post exercise mark, then declined to about half f during the

The rationale for the "Carbohydrates Addicts" diet became apparent !!

next hour. At that time the drink was consumed again and the insulin response rebounded to a level about fifty per cent (50%) higher than the first peak.

The rationale behind the carbohydrate addicts diet became apparent. "Eat anything you want in the third meal as long as it doesn't take more than one hour". You would tend to get on large spike in the insulin curve which would proceed to decline over the remaining twenty-three (23) hours, as long as you did not stimulate it again with another high carbohydrate meal or snack. Also, the spike is not likely to be large if the diet is a good mix or balanced between carbohydrate and protein. In the study cited the carbohydrate to protein ratio was 2.7: 1 which is desirable for recovery from exercise, but not desirable during your day to day activities. The Better Balanced Diet would recommend a carbohydrate to protein ratio of approximately 4 : 3.

If you are a "visual" person the following diagram (Figure 1) was created to simulate the data from the University of Texas. My contention is that most North

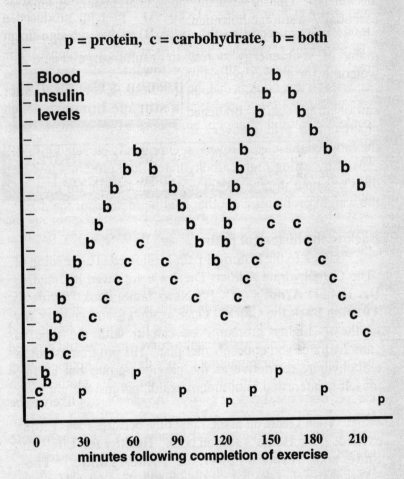

Figure 1 (adapted from Yaspelkis, et.al. Journal of Applied Physiology 75(4): 1480, 1993)

Americans stimulate the insulin spike every two hours throughout the day with high carbohydrate, low protein meals and snacks. Consequently, the insulin is forever following a progressive stair step pattern throughout the day. You might at this point ask the question - "Why is that so bad ?". The answer is - "That is what this book is all about." Insulin is essentially a storage hormone.

Following intense exercise, where you have depleted many of your energy stores, an insulin surge would be welcome for a short period of time to encourage both carbohydrate and branched chain amino acid recovery in

> **Insulin is essentially a storage hormone !!**

the fatigued muscles. However, chronically elevated insulin caused by eating high carbohydrate - low protein - low fat diets sets up a storage model which can account for many of the weight problems and other health problems of the day.

Back to the historical path

Back to the historical path I followed. The reading of "The Carbohydrate Addicts Diet" was followed by reading **Dr. Robert Arnot's** (of CBS News fame) book "**Guide to Turning Back the Clock**". Once again, I found another ally in the - "higher protein - be careful with the type of carbohydrates you choose"- diet plan. His program is not as carbohydrate restrictive as the previous group but he like myself is interested in optimum health, not just weight loss.

Then I read, all at the same time because I was getting excited, a) the **Heller's** second book "**Healthy for Life**", the **Eades** book "**Protein Power**" and **Adele Puhn's** "**The 5 Day Miracle Diet**". This time the Hellers delved into the science involved with the excess carbohydrate insulin stimulating diet as did the Eades. In fact, with both of these books, part way through the scientific reviews, I yelled "UNCLE! - enough- all-right -already -- I believe that excess insulin production is the problem. What are your solutions?" (Well maybe I wasn't quite that rattled but it was close.)

In " Healthy for Life", the Hellers promote the concept that something called "Profactor-H" (or chronic hyperinsulinemia) is responsible for excess weight gain. The Profactor - meaning 'first factor' or underlying cause, or a central imbalance that may lead to or contribute to a wide variety of disease or risk factors. They differentiate this imbalance from Profactor A which is the imbalance leading to autoimmune disorders and Profactor C which deals with abnormal cell growth leading to the series of diseases known as cancer. Unfortunately, I feel that the programs outlined in the Hellers' book are too complicated and intimidating for the average person to follow. On the positive side though, it does provide some excellent explanations of the science involved.

"Protein Power" by the husband-wife team Michael and Mary Dan Eades, who run a bariatrics practice in Little Rock, Arkansas, also elaborates on the additional health problems associated with hyperinsulinemia. The Eades diet plan would fall between Atkins (Diet Revolution)

There are additional problems associated with hyperinsulinemia !!

and Ezrin (Endocrine Control Diet) when advising on carbohydrate restriction. They recommend beginning at 30 grams of carbohydrate which is equivalent to 3 apples per day or 3 slices of whole wheat bread or 1¼ cups of cooked oatmeal. If you have a serious interest in history, read chapter two of "Protein Power" where they describe archaeological data from the ancient Egyptians which demonstrates the negative health effects of too much carbohydrate.

"The 5 - Day Miracle Diet" also eludes to the problems of high **Glycemic Index or GI** (processed carbohydrates, sugars, and starches) foods and the elevated insulin associated with these diets. Adele Puhn, a practicing nutrition consultant, offers a program although a little complicated, of frequent meals, frequent protein snacks (I like that part), lots of vegetables and a reduction of simple carbohydrates all combined with exercise and responsible supplementation. Much of her program fits very well with my thinking.   The major problem with it and many other programs is the shortfall in truly understanding good sources of complex carbohydrates. Many nutrition consultants still

recommend too many "Whole Grain Products"

Most whole grain products still have high Glycemic Index scores !!

when in fact most of these food items have high GI scores. Many of these include most cereal grain breads, breakfast cereals, crackers and pasta. Other subtle culprits include carrots, white potatoes, corn and dried fruits, particularly raisins.

The glycemic index is a relative number which describes how quickly the blood sugar rises following consumption of a food. The criterion food is simple sugar which was assigned a glycemic index (GI) of 1.00. Foods which take longer to elevate the blood sugar have a GI of less than 1.00 and a few foods have been shown to elevate the blood sugar faster than simple sugar and therefore have a GI exceeding 1.00. Apparently several breakfast cereals and that stable diet food, rice cakes, have been reported to have GI scores higher than 1.00. The GI concept was first reported by Dr. D.J.A. Jenkins and colleagues in the American Journal of Clinical Nutrition in 1981. Therefore, don't go looking for GI references in books published before that time.

My next venture was into three more recent books.

There is **Cliff Sheats "Lean Bodies"** published in 1992 where he elaborates on eating more to lose body fat. Sheats promotes a twenty-five per cent (25%) protein diet (the North American Standard recommendations range from 12- 15% with some as low as 8% in Vegetarian programs and as high as 20% in certain athletes regimens) and a serious reduction of starchy carbohydrates or high glycemic index carbohydrates. There is also an emphasis on the importance of essential fatty acids and medium chain triglycerides. Unfortunately, the Lean Bodies Program calls for only ten per cent (10%) of Calories to come from fat which is too low to get all

> **An emphasis on the importance of essential fatty acids !!**

the essential fatty acids you need. It also means that sixty-five per cent (65%) of Calories must be from the remaining macro nutrient - carbohydrates. Such high levels of carbohydrates will make it difficult to control the insulin. This is another example of an excellent idea falling short by not understanding the whole balance picture.

In 1988, **Ann Louise Gittleman**, former director of Nutrition at the Pritikin Longevity Center in Santa Monica, California, wrote a book entitled **"Beyond Pritikin"**. She describes the health problems experienced by many people, including herself, who attempted to follow the "Pritikin Program" as a life style. Gittleman demonstrated that the fat-free, high grain diets recommended in the 1970's and 1980's had temporary benefits for many, followed by health problems for many of the participants.

I personally never subscribed to the Pritikin concept as a life style because I always believed, based on good published research, that the protein and fat recommendations were far too low and actually unrealistic if not harmful. Fat does provide taste and satiety to the diet. This and other fat concepts are discussed in detail later.

Life style diets versus therapeutic diets can be an interesting discussion. It is possible that those who benefitted from the Pritikin Program initially were experiencing a therapeutic response as they readjusted their metabolism, cleansed or detoxified their systems and built certain parts of their immune systems. However, as time progressed, as it seems to do, the protein requirements

> **More protein and more essential fatty acids !!**

and essential fatty acid requirements of the hormonal, immune and muscular systems were not being met and other ailments developed. I firmly believe there is a difference between diets for corrective therapy and life style diets for optimum health. The latter requires a **"Better Balanced Diet"**.

Gittleman's other book on this subject appeared in 1996 with the title **"Your Body Knows Best"** . Here she carries on with the concepts of more protein and more essential fatty acids to aid in weight management, insulin control and consequently better health. Here programs call for twenty-five per cent (25%) of Calories to come from protein, twenty-five per cent (25%) of Calories to come from fat (good fats) and fifty per cent (50%) to come from complex (low glycemic index) carbohydrates. Exercise and responsible supplementation are also promoted.

Most recently, I was introduced to two authors who promote a diet made up of forty per cent (40%) complex carbohydrates, thirty per cent (30%) protein and thirty per cent (30%) fat (again, good fat). The first was Dr. Philip Maffetone who is well known as a fitness consultant to many superior athletes, including Mark Allen - six time winner of the Hawaiian Ironman race. Maffetone promotes "the train slow so you 'teach' your body to burn fat" concept. Apparently, if you train at an aerobic (with oxygen) intensity, you metabolize more fat and will eventually be very capable of running faster longer. I have had some personal experience with this concept, and it does work. Dr.

Train aerobically to metabolize more fat !!

Maffetone discusses the carbohydrate - insulin problems inherent in the typical North American Diet. He also promotes selective supplementation. Maffetone's books are entitled **"In Fitness and in Health"** published in 1994 and **"Training for Endurance"** published in 1996.

The other 40 - 30 - 30 contributor to the on-going discussion is **Dr. Barry Sears** who wrote **"Enter the Zone"**. This has become one of the most popular diet books in recent history, generating a huge following on the Information highway the Internet. In addition to his own web page there are literally thousands of auxiliary pages and discussion group sites emanating from all over the world. The Zone seems to be the most popular and apparently successful ventures into explaining and encouraging a dietary shift away from the processed carbohydrates mania of recent times. Again, Sears is an academic, former staff member at M.I.T in Boston, who holds patents for drug delivery control systems in cancer, aides and hormonal response therapies. He and his brother started the borage seed production movement, in Western Canada, as the best source of the essential fatty acid GLA (more about this later). I preface the discussion on the

"Zone" with this information to impress upon you that this work was developed by a credible and experienced scientist - not a clinician trying to promote his clinic. "Enter the Zone" is a book which explains, like the Hellers, Eades, Ezrin and Gittleman, the difficulties created by high carbohydrate and therefore high insulin producing diets. Sears urges the balanced diet of forty per cent (40%) carbohydrate, thirty per cent (30%) protein and thirty per cent (30%) fat and offers a system to follow to obtain this program. Unfortunately, parts of his explanations may be a little complicated and appear rigid judging from some of the comments and questions

> **That is another reason why I wrote this book !!**

generated on the Internet. In response to this, Sears has conveniently published two more books, one to help you use the diet (**"Mastering the Zone"**) and one to help you in the kitchen (**"Zone Perfect Meals in Minutes"**). That is a total of 920 pages of hard cover book material. That is another reason why I wrote this book - to provide a simplified path to the same results which is a lower carbohydrate / higher protein diet.

I have, after all this reading and some excellent experiences, chosen to subscribe to the 40 - 30 - 30 concept. The science is good, has been developing for over 100 years and I have seen very positive results in myself and others. The program recommended in this book is a combination of and an adaptation of the Zone by Dr. Sears, Protein Power by the Eades, Your Body Knows Best by Gittleman and the work of Philip Maffetone. As I mention in other places, this book is not meant to replace any of those programs but rather to help you or encourage to get with a "40 - 30 - 30" program. As the expression goes -**JUST GET WITH THE PROGRAM**-- Hopefully the rationale is clear and the directions simple enough to help anyone get started. If you are a connoisseur of scientific knowledge and you are looking for more elaborate and complete menus and recipes, please refer to these four books, plus "Mastering the Zone and "Zone Perfect Meals in Minutes".

Why did I go through this historical stuff ??

Why did I go through all of this historical stuff?? The major reason was to impress upon you that:

    a) the information on the reduced carbohydrate concept is not new.

    b) the science behind the concept is considerable and sound.

and   c) properly managed, the concept works to provide responsible weight management and pathways to better health.

I hope I have succeeded in reaching that objective. The question now is -- **Are you convinced?**

    I previously mentioned that many dietary extremes have their converts who were returned to health by 'fruit only at breakfast' or 'ten per cent (10%) fat diets' or 'high fiber diets, high complex carbohydrate, low Calorie diets'. The list of extremes goes on and on. The reality is that there is no single diet suitable for all mankind. There are genetic components which have developed over thousands of years of evolution or adaptation (whatever you want to call it). There are trends that call for dietary differences between Eskimos, Northern Europeans and Equatorial dwellers. Some very interesting reading is the material on blood types which reflect ancestry, adaptation (evolution) and dietary needs. The work by the D'Adamos, a father and son pair, deals with this concept in a book "The D'Adamo Diet" published in 1989 and in a series of publications 1991-1993. A discussion of this topic exceeds the scope of this book, but I wanted to acknowledge the existence of this material.

If your health has been impaired and your body fat is in excess due to a poorly balanced or incomplete diet, it may take more than a return to a balanced diet to correct the abnormalities. You may have to over-correct for a period time. Hence we have the reported successes of several "dietary extremes" but they are usually of value for one to three years after which new problems may arise. Gittleman discusses this well in "Beyond Pritikin".

I recommend a program, consistent with "the Zone" dietary plan but with an emphasis on slightly more protein (see the chapter 'Protein is the Answer') and I

I am more aggressive with supplementation !!

am more aggressive with supplementation and not as fussy about the saturated fat issue as long as the essential fatty acids are in abundant supply. The essential fatty acid issue is discussed in some detail by Sears in "Enter The Zone" but it is probably best covered by **Udo Erasmus** in his book **"Fats the Heal and Fats that Kill"**. The Eades in "Protein Power" also support my position on higher levels of protein consumption for most people. Aerobic (fat burning) exercise is a part of the package, consistent with Maffetone's work and I urge a higher fibre diet with responsible and considerable supplementation. This is also explained in chapter 9, "The Stuff You Are Not Eating", later in this book.

5

TECHNICAL STUFF

One short coming of most diet books I have read has been a reluctance to explain some of the fundamental biochemistry - physiology of fat digestion, absorption, storage and utilization. The popular concept is that "Fat goes from your lips to your hips", therefore, avoid fat! This paradigm is the foundation of the controversy or criticism of reduced carbohydrate eating plans. The purpose of this chapter is to hopefully explain, in reasonably simple terms, how fat does go from your lips to all parts of the body and back out as an energy source. To verify most of this chapter the **Fat digestion occurs in** skeptics may read any recent **the small intestine !!** comprehensive book on human physiology or biochemistry.

Digestion

Fat digestion occurs in the **small intestine** in the presence of bile or bile salts produced from cholesterol by the **liver** and released by the **gall bladder**. The scheme looks something like this:

Fat + bile + agitation = **emulsified fat** + lipase = **60% fatty acids and glycerol and 40% mono & di glycerides**

Bile salts progressively emulsify fat globules into smaller and smaller particles so the enzymes known as **Lipase,** which are water soluble and attack the fats from the surface only, can further alter the fat into useful biochemical components.

```
        H
  H - C - OH
  H - C - OH
  H - C - OH        or the formula   $C_6H_{12}O_6$
  H - C - OH              represents **glucose**
  H - C - OH
  H - C - OH
        H
```

```
        H
  H - C - OH
  H - C - OH        or the formula        $C_3H_8O3$
  H - C - OH              represents **glycerol**
        H
```

(notice that glycerol = approximately ½ a glucose molecule)

```
        H
  H - C - Fatty Acid
  H - C - OH        represents a **mono-glyceride**
  H - C - OH
        H
```

```
        H
  H - C - Fatty Acid
  H - C - Fatty Acid
  H - C - OH  represents a **di-glyceride**
        H
```

Glycerol is essentially one half (½) of a glucose molecule, a mono glyceride is the 3 carbon glycerol with one fatty acid attached, the di-glyceride has two fatty acids attached and logically the tri-glyceride has three fatty acids.

Absorption

Fats are believed to be absorbed through the intestinal walls in the form

Fat dissolves into the intestinal wall !!

of fatty acids, some monoglycerides and a few di-glycerides. The mechanism of absorption appears to be:

a) Fatty acids dissolve into the cell of the membrane of the intestinal wall.

b) Fatty acids combine with CoEnzyme A in these cells (at Endoplasmic Reticulum level, for the physiologists) with the help of energy

c) Fatty acids plus CoEnzyme-A combine with glycerol, monoglycerides or diglycerides **in the membrane of these cells** to become triglycerides

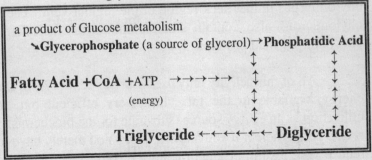

a product of Glucose metabolism

↘Glycerophosphate (a source of glycerol)**→Phosphatidic Acid**

Fatty Acid +CoA +ATP →→→→→→

(energy)

Triglyceride ←←←←←← **Diglyceride**

The Triglycerides are deposited by the membrane cells into the **submucosal fluids** in the form of little (0.5 microns) fat droplets, coated in protein which allows the droplet to remain suspended in body fluids. These droplets, referred to as **chylomicrons** are picked up by the lymphatic system and pumped into the blood veins at the thoracic duct (jugular vein in the neck region). Apparently eighty to ninety per cent (80 - 90%) of all fat absorbed from the gut reaches the blood in this manner. The other ten to twenty percent (10 - 20%) is absorbed directly into the liver's portal blood before it is converted to a triglyceride. In general, the medium and short chain

fatty **Most dietary fat starts as triglycerides !!**

acids

can be absorbed this way (i.e. butter fat). This may account for some reported success using Medium Chain fatty acids as an efficient source of energy (see **Sheats "Lean Bodies"**). I do know two cross country skiers, during a recent North Pole expedition used ¼pound sticks of butter to supply additional energy during their grueling sojourn.

To summarize to this point - most dietary fat which starts as triglycerides, is digested into fatty acids, in the small intestine, absorbed by the cells of the intestinal wall, converted back into triglycerides, released into body fluids, picked up by the Lymph and dispersed into the blood as chylomicrons in the neck region of the jugular vein. These chylomicrons also contain small amounts of cholesterol, phospholipids and proteins.

All of this activity only uses four per cent (4%) of the energy available in the fat. It is very efficient but fat utilization as an energy source (substrate for the biochemists) is also very efficient if you allow it to be. You merely have to reduce your insulin production and / or raise your glucagon production by either eating fewer carbohydrates and eating more protein. or increasing exercise.

Assimilation

Fat (triglycerides) is removed from the blood by:

a) hydrolysis (removal of Hydrogen ions) of the chylomicron triglycerides by an enzyme Lipoprotein Lipase. (see next flow chart)

or b) absorbed as a whole chylomicron by the liver cells and either metabolized for energy or converted to other lipid substances the body needs.

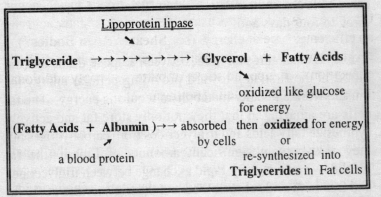

That, in a 'nutshell' is a summary of how fat goes from food to cell storage, known as **adipose tissue**. The adipose tissue is usually called the fat deposits or fat depots. The major function of adipose tissue is storage of triglycerides until they are needed for energy. A subsidiary function is to conserve body heat by acting as insulation.

The fat cells of adipose tissue are known as modified fibroblasts and are capable of storing pure triglycerides in quantities equal to ninety per cent (90%) of their volume. The triglycerides in storage are in liquid form and it has been shown that with prolonged exposure to cold, the fatty acids become shorter or less saturated, making it easier to remain liquid and thus available for hydrolysis - the first step in metabolize more fat.

Just because the fatty acids have arrived in the adipose tissue and occupied ninety per cent of the volume of the cells in this tissue, does not mean it stays there. In fact, there is considerable evidence that the fatty acids **turn-over** rate in adipose tissue is very fast and regular. Apparently the fat you carry today is completely different from the fat you carried three to four days ago.

> **Fatty Acid turnover rate is very fast !!**

Exchanging stored fat between adipose tissue and the blood is the first step toward providing cellular energy for muscle work and other metabolism requiring energy. The fat cells are amazing in that they not only store fat and actively synthesize fatty acids and triglycerides from carbohydrates but they also contain significant amounts of Lipase (the fat breakdown enzyme) for rapid exchange between triglycerides and free fatty acids of the blood and the triglycerides of the fat cells. Obviously there is more to discuss and it is obviously more complicated than the simplistic statement that "fat goes from your lips to your hips".

Utilization

A small and highly variable quantity of fatty acids are always present in the blood, usually in combination with the blood protein albumin. Because fatty acids ionize strongly in water (i.e. body fluids), upon their release into the blood the ionized fatty acids combine with albumin and we call them **Free Fatty Acids** (FFA's). Another name is 'non-esterified' fatty acids to distinguish them from other fatty acids transported in smaller amounts as esters of glycerol, cholesterol, etc.

The FFA concentration is around 15 mg / 100 ml of blood for a total of 0.75 grams in the entire circulatory system. Interesting, though is the fact that this small amount accounts for most of the transport of fats from one part of the body to another. Such an occurrence is possible because of the rapid "turnover" rate of fatty acids. One half of the fatty acid is replaced by new fatty acid every two to three minutes. Therefore, the calculations show that over half of all the energy required by the body can be provided this way without increasing blood fatty acid levels.

All the conditions that increase the rate of fat utilization for energy will also increase the fatty acid concentration in the blood (by up to ten fold). This is particularly true in starvation, low carbohydrate diets or in Type I

Most dietary fat by-passes the liver through the lymph !!

Diabetes where low insulin levels and or availability of carbohydrates for cellular energy are restricted.

One must understand that most of the dietary fat by-passes the liver through the lymph on the way to storage. But, over fifty per cent (50%) of endogenous (from inside the cell) fat, mobilized for energy metabolism, starts its degradation in the liver. The blood triglycerides, released from cells with the aid of tissue lipase, travel through the liver where they are hydrolyzed into FFA's and glycerol. The glycerol is metabolized like glucose whereas the FFA's follow a series of degradation steps by combining with CoEnzyme A. This multi step process is known as Beta oxidation. It is the process whereby FFA's become Acetyl CoEnzyme A (Acetyl Co-A) which enters the same oxidative pathway as Glucose and produces useful energy. With the liver so involved with

Co-A) which enters the same oxidative pathway as Glucose and produces useful energy. With the liver so involved with this process, it cannot use all of the Acetyl Co-A for itself so it allows two molecules to combine in pairs and become Acetoacetic acid which freely diffuses into the blood and into the

Acetoacetic acid accumulation is known as Ketosis !!

body tissues in need of energy. Once in tissue cells, the acetoacetic acid splits and is available for oxidation as Acetyl Co-A just as glucose would be. (see the next diagram)

Usually the level of acetoacetic acid in the blood remains below 3 mg / 100 ml (3 mg%). Despite small quantities in the blood, tremendous amounts are actually moved from fat cells to liver to working cells.

When large quantities of acetoacetic acid do accumulate in the blood, it is known as **Ketosis**. This can occur during starvation, in Diabetes Mellitus (Type I), or when the diet is primarily fat or extremely low in carbohydrate. In these latter states, virtually no carbohydrate is metabolized either because none is available or there is no insulin available to transport the glucose.

A lack if available carbohydrate automatically increases the rate of removal of fatty acids from adipose tissue. Several other hormonal factors like, an increase in glucocorticoids from the adrenal gland and a decrease in insulin production from the pancreas and an increase in glucagon also from the pancreas, will enhance fatty acid mobilization from fat stores. Under these extremes the virtual quantity of acetoacetic acid pouring out of the liver exceeds

Liver Enzymes

hydrolysis
in Liver

Triglycerides→↕→**Glycerol** →→**Glyceraldehyde** →→ **Glucose**
(normal
energy path)
↕
↕ enzymes
↕
↕

step ① **FFA's + CoA +ATP**→→**Fatty acyl Co-A +AMP +P**
(energy)

-a series of degradations with enzymes and flavoproteins -

step ⑤ Surplus
Acetyl Co-A →→**Acetoacetic Acid** →→→ diffuses easily
into blood

once in cells - separates into **2 Acetyl Co-A**→→Glucose energy
path

Surplus **Acetoacetic Acid**→→**Acetone & Beta Hydroxy butyric
Acid**
(Ketone bodies)

even what normal cells can oxidize unless there is considerable physical exercise (high level of energy expenditure) included. The concentration of acetoacetic acid can increase to thirty (30) times normal which could lead to considerable acidosis. However, acetoacetic acid can be converted to two other compounds, one is an acid (Beta-hydroxybutyric Acid) and the other is acetone. These two substances and acetoacetic acid have become known as **Ketone Bodies** or **Ketones**. Ketone excretion can contribute to temporary body and breath odor. But, if one changes their diet slowly from high carbohydrate to low carbohydrate and higher fat, Ketosis usually doesn't occur. Ketones can either be picked up and metabolized for energy or expelled through normal elimination procedures. A simple tool known as the "Keto stick" is used to test the presence of Ketones in the urine and is recommended in the Atkin's diet. If Ketones are expelled then they have not been metabolized for energy which can account for weight loss that does not match the conventional arithmetic of Calories spent.

> **Ketone excretion can lead to body and breath odor !!**

In the fasting individual, cellular fuel obviously must be obtained from available energy in the form of stored material in the body. In the development of the ideal energy stores for the mobile animal, such as man, nature has to meet a number requirements. For reasons of portability, each molecule should carry a large amount of energy per unit of weight. The material should be fitted into various oddly shaped spaces and compartments of the body. It should possess a great storage stability and, at the same time, be readily available, capable of being rapidly converted into oxidizable substrate when needed, without being spontaneously explosive.

It has been pointed many times that the above list of requirements are met remarkably well by our fat storage / release mechanisms. Fat has a high energy content, (9 Calories per gram compared to 4 Calories per gram for carbohydrates) and is stable, yet readily mobilized. The efficiency of fat as a storage method for reserve energy is further enhanced by existing in liquid droplets, whereas carbohydrates require a great deal of water (almost 3 grams per gram of stored carbohydrate) when in storage.

Different animal species have adapted their energy store to their own particular needs. In most animals, the energy for high intensity muscular effort is obtained largely by metabolizing carbohydrate: but hydrated (with water) glycogen is a very heavy fuel compares with fat and in the locust which **Fat is also an important energy source !!** flies great distances a sufficient load of glycogen would severely limit range and endurance. The locust adapted by developing a system which rapidly transforms carbohydrate into fat, which alone is used during flight. Similarly in, migrating salmon and the eel and birds, fat also constitutes the main source of energy.

In the past, however, it has been generally assumed that the main and primary energy source during muscular work or exercise in mammals was carbohydrate, and that fat was only reserve fuel used mainly at rest and during recovery. Recent research has clearly established that fat also is an important source of energy fuel for the working muscle, and that the percentage participation of fat and carbohydrate in the metabolic mixture depends on a number factors, including the severity and duration of the work in relation to subject's maximal aerobic power and the diet.

During intense exercise, a maximum of 3 grams of carbohydrate may be utilized during every minute of exercise in one with a very high aerobic power. Therefore, blood glucose can only cover a few minutes of intense work (circulating blood glucose adds up to approximately 20 grams in total). The central nervous system (brain & spinal cord) depends to a very great extent on circulating blood glucose for it's energy production. To prevent a marked decrease in the blood glucose levels, some sort of barrier must exist to stop all of the circulating glucose from entering the muscle cells and thus creating a condition known as hypoglycemia (low blood sugar).

The permeability of the cell membrane for glucose depends on the blood insulin concentrations which falls during heavy exercise. Second certain enzymes are necessary for the uptake of glucose across the membrane and at least one such enzyme (hexokinase) is inhibited by products from the breakdown of glycogen (storage form of glucose in muscles and liver). Consequently the muscles will use muscle glycogen directly for an energy substrate and not circulating blood glucose. Actually, very little muscle glycogen ever returns to become circulating blood glucose. This fact is important when one considers the implications of an elevated carbohydrate intake. Once muscle glycogen stores are full, the only way they become depleted is for that particular muscle to metabolize the muscle glycogen. The muscle glycogen store in the quadriceps (front thigh) muscle never

Muscle glycogen rarely returns as blood glucose !!

moves via the blood glucose route to become blood sugar nor muscle glycogen in the biceps (front to upper arm) muscles.

The relative contribution of carbohydrate oxidation to total metabolism increases as a curvilinear function of exercise intensity up until approximately the point of Maximal oxygen intake at which time glucose becomes the sole energy substrate. During light exercise, there is a gradual increase in the absolute amount of fat oxidized as aerobic endurance exercise progresses. In this latter situation, fatty acids can serve as the primary fuel source, which allows for very prolonged activity, such as walking, even when in the fasted state. The maximal utilization of fatty acids in the untrained individual may occur at about fifty per cent (50%) of maximal oxygen intake levels. The higher the exercise intensities, the reliance on fatty acids declines and the reliance on carbohydrates increases. Even at relatively high exercise intensities, fatty acids remain as an important secondary fuel

> **Fatty acids can serve as the primary fuel source !!**

acting as a muscle glycogen sparing mechanism and thus prolonging the ability to exercise. This is discussed further in the chapter on exercise.

Carbohydrates to Triglycerides

I felt it necessary to conclude this chapter with a brief explanation of how carbohydrates become fat! When there are more carbohydrates available than can be used immediately for energy or stored in the form of glycogen, the excess is rapidly converted into triglycerides and the stored in the adipose tissue. It is now understood that this fat synthesis process takes place primarily in the cells themselves and only a small amount is converted by the liver. Older textbooks emphasized the liver as the major conversion site. Regardless of where the conversion takes place, the triglycerides still end up in the adipose tissue. This conversion of carbohydrates is complicated and not totally understood yet.

In simplistic terms, surplus glucose is converted via the normal glycolytic metabolic pathway to glycerophosphate and Acetyl Co-A. The Acetyl Co-A is converted to Malonyl Co-A and in the presence of significant energy, 1 Acetyl Co-A and 8 Malonyl Co-A molecules combine to form Fatty Acids. Naturally there are many intermediate enzymes involved in these functions and the pancreatic hormone insulin is essential to move the glucose into the cells where all this takes place. The conversion is fairly efficient, using only fifteen per cent (15%) of the available energy in the glucose. The remaining energy is stored in the triglycerides.

Most significant to the theme of this book is for you to understand that once the liver and muscle glycogen stores are full, any surplus carbohydrate, which is in the form of blood glucose by now, will be converted to triglycerides unless needed immediately for physical activity. The liver will hold approximately eighty to ninety (80-90) grams of glycogen and the muscles will hold another three hundred to four hundred

> **Muscles can store a mere 300 to 400 grams of glycogen, representing up to 1600 Calories !!**

(300 - 400) grams which all adds up to approximately 1960 Calories at the most. If you do not metabolize those Calories immediately, then they will be converted to fat. You also need to understand that it would be impossible to metabolize one hundred per cent (100%) of those glycogen Calories without exhausting one hundred per cent of your muscles. Therefore, as you go through your day eating a relatively high carbohydrate diet, there is likely to be a net inflow of fat. The only way to mobilize fat from storage is to reduce insulin and increase glucagon production from the pancreas. This will be difficult to do in the typical pattern of eating an insulin stimulating meal or snack every two hours throughout the day. By the way, coffee contributes to this insulin elevation by stimulating the liver to release glucose into the blood stream.

My major reason for writing this chapter was to

impress upon you that fat is and excellent source of energy, particularly during moderate exercise and it is very readily available. The second point to be reinforced is that surplus glucose from carbohydrate consumption is easily converted to fat in storage and difficult to remove as long as one continues to eat surplus carbohydrates. The 40 - 30 - 30 ratio of carbohydrates to protein and fat is designed to help you remove from storage and metabolize fat.

Surplus glucose will be converted to fat !!

6

INSULIN-GOOD GUY / BAD GUY!

Unless you have been living in a cave for the past seventy-five years, you are aware that insulin, a hormone secreted by the pancreas, is necessary to control blood sugar levels. You also likely know that a Diabetic, one who suffers from sugar diabetes, is one whose blood sugar (glucose) remains elevated which means the sugar is not reaching the intended cells to be metabolized

> **Obviously, insulin is a very necessary hormone !!**

into energy or converted and stored as fat. Many of you also know that there are basically two types of diabetes. Type I diabetes or diabetes mellitus, or juvenile diabetes is due to the inability of the pancreas to produce and secrete enough insulin. Type II diabetes, diabetes insipidus, or adult onset diabetes occurs when the insulin receptor sites on the cells of the body resist accepting insulin, rendering it non-functional. Consequently, blood sugar and blood insulin levels remain elevated.

Obviously, insulin is a very necessary hormone with many healthy, life giving functions. Controlling blood sugar traffic is only one of those functions. It has been referred to as a product of the "thrifty gene". That would be a genetic tendency to have the pancreas secrete extra insulin or surplus insulin, when stimulated by the presence of glucose (the primary sugar in the blood), so the body may send this sugar into storage. Storage in the form of muscle glycogen (glucose stored in muscle), liver glycogen and body fat. These genetics evolved or adapted through the "survival of the fittest" tendencies of earlier times when man did not have the convenience and guarantee of three meals every day. Consequently, when food was unavailable for short to longer periods of time, insulin was not produced in significant quantity. Instead, the pancreas would produce and release glucagon, a hormone responsible for mobilizing stored fat and making it available for energy.

Insulin levels in the blood control and counter balance blood glucagon concentrations. The ongoing balancing act between insulin and glucagon, both produced by the pancreas in

> **Rate of increase in blood glucose is the operative word !!**

response to the rate of increase or decrease in blood glucose levels, virtually rules your life. **Rate of increase** in blood glucose levels is the operative word here. That is why high glycemic index foods cause so many problems with this balance and leads to hyperinsulinemia which leads to fat storage and other hormonal imbalances. The function of these two pancreatic hormones and how the cells respond determines your level of alertness, energy and numerous other body functions which are about to be outlined.

The awareness of the body's sensitivity to the balance or imbalance of pancreatic hormones was eluded to in 1936 by Dr. H.P.Himsworth in a paper published in Lancet. This issue reached a new level of seriousness in 1989, when Dr. G.M.Reaven published his work in The Journal of Diabetes, entitled "Role of Insulin Resistance in Human Disease". Modern and sophisticated technology needed to develop before Dr. Himsworth's work could be readdressed. The early term used in these studies was "hyperinsulinemia" which translated meant 'too much insulin in the blood'.

Initially it was perceived as some anomaly by the pancreas, fairly common, and treated by attempting to treat the symptoms. It was not well understood until an explosion of research papers linking **"hyperinsulinemia"** hyperinsulinemia with many other disease conditions were published. This research explosion was made possible by the introduction of the computer. In recent years, huge data base studies involving the collection of a wide range of data on large populations over longer periods of time, have emerged. These data bases allowed for the quick analysis of an infinite number of correlations. When significant correlations between two or more variables are located it can become a jump-start for further research. It becomes even more intensive when several data bases report similar correlations. However, in another part of this book I reviewed the cautions which must be exercised in correlation based studies. Remember, correlation does not mean causation. So the new research following the discovery of significant correlation involves the development of logical explanations through animal and clinical (human) research. This latter phase is where the current exciting research into insulin production / response is developing and it seems to be exploding a few myths.

Elevated insulin response can be the result of either
a) an over-production by the pancreas as it responds to the elevation of the blood sugar

or   b) cellular receptor resistance to insulin which may be linked to chronic glucose elevation and the attempt to transport the glucose into the active tissue cells. The Hellers referred to the elevated insulin as **"Profactor H"**. They propose that profactor H is caused by one of two cofactors or a combination of the two cofactors. Cofactors are contributors to a final result. **Cofactor P** refers to the over-production of insulin by the pancreas and **cofactor R** is the resistance to insulin by the metabolically active cells. This cofactor has previously been referred to as **"insulin resistance"**, **"carbohydrate intolerance"**, **"glucose intolerance"** and **"glucose, insulin, or carbohydrate insensitivity"**.

Profactor H - cofactor P, cofactor R !!

The pancreas releases or secretes insulin in response to the presence of glucose in the blood stream. Insulin secretion is more dramatic (rises proportionally more) when the blood glucose level rises quickly. In other words the response is more sensitive to rate of increase than to the absolute level. Consequently, foods which digest quickly tend to raise blood glucose more quickly and produced an exaggerated insulin production response. This is known as the Glycemic Index (GI) referred to and explained in chapter four, page 38.

It should now become evident that a single fasting level of blood insulin would not be a very reliable test for excess insulin production. Insulin dynamics must be considered before clinical evaluation can occur and it may be that physiological responses in the form of symptoms may be the most reliable tool here.

If the cause of elevated insulin is cofactor P, the body's response would be that of the conventional hypoglycemic. Hypoglycemia is characterized by strong cravings for carbohydrate rich food followed in one to two hours with fatigue, the 'shakes', headaches, sleepiness, irritability and weakness. The elevated insulin, in response to the carbohydrate food intake, has disposed of the blood sugar into storage and inhibited glucagon production which prevents fat mobilization for energy and the consequence is fatigue and lack of control. These symptoms subside or reverse with a 'fix' of carbohydrate, further inhibiting fat mobilization - the physiological reason for the morning and afternoon "coffee break" at work. Coffee breaks usually

> **These symptoms subside with a carbohydrate "fix" !!**

follow a meal by one and a half to two (1½ - 2) hours. Oh yes, where does all this energy giving carbohydrate (blood glucose) go particularly in a relatively sedentary individual? The answer is, to fat storage.

If the cause of elevated insulin is that of cellular resistance, the glucose never reaches the cells and the insulin continues to rise as the pancreas attempts to complete its job. One of the satiety (satisfaction of hunger) centres or regulators is blood insulin levels. Elevated insulin can signal the body to eat. The resistor is likely to be diagnosed as a Type II diabetic because the glucose does not leave the blood stream. Hence one has elevated blood sugar similar the Type I diabetic (caused by under-production of insulin). Unfortunately the Type II diabetic or borderline Type II diabetic with their insatiable hunger, elevated insulin (the storage hormone) and consequently depressed glucagon (the fat mobilizing hormone) will tend to gain weight as the surplus glucose is converted to triglycerides for storage.

Insulin, the Good Guy !

Insulin "the good guy" is responsible for controlling blood sugar and direct fat storage. Operating under the control of the "thrifty gene", it allows us to store some of the excess food (actually **'all'** of the excess) as muscle glycogen, liver glycogen and triglycerides. As stated before, the triglycerides are the major components of adipose tissue. When food is not available and blood sugar decreases, the pancreas secretes glucagon which mobilizes fat stored and encourages the liver to engage in "gluconeogenesis" (the

Insulin also directs amino acid and fatty acid flow !!

making of new glucose-- gluco means glucose, neo means new and genesis means to make) and helps to restore energy sources to the active tissue. It is a good system when it is kept in balance.

Insulin also directs amino acid flow and fatty acid flow which means it has an anabolic (growth) effect by providing materials to tired muscles and allowing them to repair and increase in size. Cholesterol synthesis is also controlled - in part - by insulin as is appetite and fluid retention through optimizing kidney function.

At "normal" concentrations, insulin helps to decrease blood glucose and increase blood protein levels, both stimulate the release of Growth Hormone. You will also have an increase in human growth hormone production observing a reduced carbohydrate diet, increased protein intake, decreased "bad" fat consumption -(trans fatty acids, and PGE_2 forming fats), increased essential fatty acid intake, particularly the "activated" essential fatty acids known as GLA and EPA, and an increase in exercise intensity.

Insulin, the Bad Guy !

Insulin, as a problem, occurs when production appears to be excess (cofactor P) or insulin resistance has developed (cofactor R) and the blood insulin levels remain elevated for long periods of time. Chronically or frequently elevated insulin causes the kidneys to retain sodium throughout the body, which results in fluid retention (to dilute the sodium) which in turn produces an increase in blood volume which in turn causes a rise in blood pressure.

The growth hormone action of insulin can "backfire" !!

The growth hormone action of insulin can also back fire by producing more cells in the smooth muscle wall of arteries , making them less elastic and providing less "give" during the systolic pressure stroke by the heart producing an elevated blood pressure.

A third way elevated insulin raises blood pressure is by stimulating the nervous system to release adrenaline-like hormones (norepinephrine, the same hormones released in time of stress) which increases blood pressure and heart rate.

Elevated insulin causes an increase in cholesterol production that is not all bad news. Since cholesterol is a necessary component of all cell walls and is the precursor to bile production along with many other hormones, it would be a mistake to stop all cholesterol production. However, the excess production of low density cholesterol (LDL- the bad cholesterol) stimulated by insulin will inhibit the production of high density cholesterol (HDL - the good cholesterol). HDL cholesterol acts to scavenge LDL and return it to the liver for disposal. High levels of LDL become susceptible to oxidation and free radical formation which is when it causes all the artery muscle wall damage leading to heart disease. Remember, that the amount of cholesterol in the blood stream has relatively little to do with how much cholesterol you eat. Blood cholesterol levels are much more affected by insulin levels in response to carbohydrate consumption than by the amount of cholesterol consumed.

A third and possibly the most recognized role of excess insulin is that of fat storage. As the storage hormone, elevated insulin is very busy converting "excess" carbohydrates

> **Blood cholesterol doesn't directly reflect cholesterol eaten !!**

and proteins into fatty acids, uniting them with half a sugar molecule (glycerol) and storing it all as fat (adipose tissue).

Finally, the least obvious but possibly the most significant malfunction created by excess insulin is that of creating an imbalance in the **eicosanoids** (super hormones) of the body. These specialized, very transient hormone-like substances control every delicate body function in some way. I mention transient because we do not store these compounds but make them as we need them. They include the prostaglandins (the best known members of the group), the prostacyclins, thrombaxanes and the leukotrienes. Eicosanoids (pronounced 'I - cose - an - oids') control inflammation, blood pressure, blood clotting, most of the immune system, sexual potency, much of our pain (which may be inflammation related), fever, digestion, constriction of and dilation of lung airways and blood vessels.

One of the major principles behind Dr. Sears now famous "Zone" diet is all centred on eicosanoid production and balance. When this production, primarily from the essential fatty acids, and balance is achieved you are in the "Zone" and "all" your body functions - physical - mental - emotional - will operate at an optimal level. Too much insulin seems to be the largest inhibitor to achieving this state.

To Summarize

Insulin levels in the blood stream virtually control your life! Insulin is absolutely necessary, you cannot live without it! Insulin controls blood sugar, directs fat storage, directs amino acid flow, directs fatty acid flow and cholesterol synthesis by the

> **Essential fatty acids affect - the physical, the mental and the emotional components of life !!**

liver. It functions as a growth hormone, appetite controller and regulator of body fluids through its influence on the kidneys. However, excess insulin, either from over-production (cofactor P) or cellular resistance (cofactor R) can create havoc with your metabolism. Excess insulin causes:

a) an increase in fat production(from carbohydrates) and fat storage.

b) over-production of LDL cholesterol (bad).

c) an increase in sodium retention by the kidneys, resulting in fluid retention and elevated blood pressure.

d) an increase in arterial smooth muscle wall growth contributing to less elastic arteries, leading to elevated blood pressure.

e) an inhibitory effect on pancreatic glucagon production leading to less gluconeogenesis and less fat mobilization.

and f) an imbalance in eicosanoid production by increasing the negative eicosanoids and decreasing the production of good eicosanoids from the essential fatty acids resulting in a myriad of imbalances and ill health.

One final note to observe. It is not enough to measure

the fasting level of insulin in the blood in an attempt to diagnose this condition. True, if the fasting level of insulin is chronically elevated over several tests, it can become grounds for further investigation. Unfortunately, the level of insulin is a result of either how the pancreas behaves in response to certain carbohydrates or how

There is no drug to control insulin production !!

resistant the cell receptors have become as a result of constant insulin bombardment. Therefore, it becomes a matter of assessing the response to carbohydrate intake. In other words, as I mentioned elsewhere in this book, "Symptoms are always approximately right". A symptoms evaluation is a good idea to help assess the severity of the response and therefore how rigid your diet should be. Further discussion on this matter appears in Heller's book **"Healthy for Life"** on pages 45 to 47.

You must also realize that there is no drug to reduce insulin. You can only reduce your insulin level by reducing you carbohydrate consumption.

7

PROTEIN IS THE ANSWER

As the word "Protein" - meaning 'to come first', from the Greek word "Protos"- suggests, protein has been recognized since early times to be absolutely essential for life. We know that some fatty acids

"Protein " meaning 'to come first'!!

are also essential and some carbohydrate is desirable but never proven to be essential (there this no RDA / RNI for carbohydrate). We recognize some dietary requirement for approximately thirty-five (35) vitamins and minerals but not for carbohydrate. Even primitive man (the nomads) followed their protein food sources. Most North Americans plan their meals around the protein source and not the carbohydrate source with exception of some pasta meals. Restaurant menus are categorized by protein source and protein usually commands a large share of our food budgets. The primacy of protein persists. Protein rich foods are generally preferred, likely because most protein rich foods are also excellent sources of other essential nutrients.

Every day, your body builds and loses millions of cells. We need protein to replace the lost cells. Now it is true that when cells breakdown into their components, not all of the material is lost or excreted or metabolized, but some is. Some of the amino acids (building blocks of protein) are recycled into new cells, but many are excreted or metabolized for energy, depending on physical demands placed on these cells. Protein is found in every cell in the body. There are thousands of different specific proteins throughout the body.

With the exception of water, there is more protein in your body than anything else. A 160 pound man is made up of more than thirty (30) pounds of protein.

It greatly concerns me that protein is the most abused macro nutrient in our diets. For some reason the standard dietary phrases associated with protein recommendations go like this: "North Americans have too much protein in their diets; or North Americans get adequate protein; or too much protein can be dangerous, causing kidney and

> **It greatly concerns me that protein is the most abused macro nutrient!!**

liver damage; or too much protein will cause osteoporosis by leaching calcium from the bones". These statements will be addressed in this chapter.

I learned a great deal about protein through my experience as a beef cattle rancher. Research in the livestock industry has demonstrated very clearly that adequate protein is essential for optimum reproduction, growth and milk production which are all signs of good health and productivity in the animals which, by the way, are all mammals. Livestock producers do not take protein consumption for granted - they test all feed for protein content. **Optimum health is dependent upon consumption of adequate, high quality, complete protein**.

Protein is significant because it is :

a) necessary for life;
b) necessary for growth;
c) part of every cell;
d) needed to replace cells;
e) needed to repair tissue;
f) a source of energy;

g) a major part of every hormone;

h) a major part of the immune system;

i) a major part of every enzyme;

j) a major part of reproductive physiology.

With so many significant and vital functions for protein, why would we ever take it for granted or risk not consuming enough? For the above reasons, the **Better Balanced Diet**, the Zone Diet, the Eades in their "Protein Power" book all use the 'protein first' criteria to design their eating plans. In the "Let's Eat" chapter we begin by establishing your protein requirement and build the carbohydrates and fat requirements around the protein.

> **A meal or snack relatively high in protein will increase your level of alertness !!**

Did you know that a meal or snack that is relatively high in protein will increase your level of alertness? On the opposite side, a meal relatively high in carbohydrate will calm you, make you sleepy or even sluggish. Doesn't it make sense therefore to remain alert throughout your waking hours? You achieve this state by **eating protein in every meal and every snack.** As an advocate of the 40 - 30 - 30 food selection plan, previously described, I am not advocating a high protein or an excess protein diet. Rather I advocate enough protein to meet the stressful demands, both physical and mental, of the modern world. The protein recommendations in this book are higher than most conventional diet plans but not as high as some of more radical body building diet regimens.

Protein Deficiency

Symptoms of protein deficiency or protein energy malnutrition (PEM) include a weakened immune system, loss of muscle mass, hair loss, inflammatory conditions, poor digestion, low sperm count and even yeast infections.

Weakened immune systems can account for innumerable disease conditions ranging from bacterial and viral infections to allergies. Dr. Sherwood L. Gorbach of Tufts University School of Medicine reported in the December 1992 issue of Nutrition Reviews, that PEM can disturb normal bowel flora. He indicated that bacterial

PEM can disturb normal bowel flora !!

overgrowth in the intestinal system is seen with even moderate protein energy malnutrition. I would suggest that this could partially account for yeast infection (Candida Albicans) epidemic raging throughout North America. We also know that a yeast infection is allowed to flourish when the immune system is weak and such infections are encouraged when refined carbohydrates are in abundance.

According to Dr. Willard Krehl, the former editor in chief of the American Journal of Clinical Nutrition, in a paper distributed by Vitamin Nutrition Information Services (VNIS) in Nutley, N.J., protein energy malnutrition has been seen in forty-four per cent (44%) of the hospitalized population. I would hope that is part the reason for the hospital visit and that the deficiency did not commence after entering the hospital. Dr. Krehl added that this deficiency leaves the patient in double jeopardy. "Their disease or injury dramatically increases their nutritional needs, even to the point of precipitating malnutrition which in turn impairs the immune response and the ability the heal".

Three other groups of people tend to show protein malnutrition. The first is the "diet for weight loss" group. I have always contended that most weight loss diets do not possess enough protein. Aversion to high protein foods in weight loss menus comes from the mistaken conclusion that these foods contain too much fat and

Protein and Fat control appetite !!

we must reduce that fat. Well, the result is very poor satiety control. Protein and fat control appetite over a long period of time whereas carbohydrates, particularly refined carbohydrates, leave the gut quickly, stimulate the insulin production mechanisms and find their way into storage in less than two hours, leaving one hungry again. Because many higher protein foods carry fat they have been unnecessarily excluded from many weight loss programs. If you want to control your appetite, be sure there is **protein in every meal and every snack.** (I cannot make this statement often enough)

The second group of protein malnourished people are the high performance athletes. Symptoms indicating this are:

a) athletes contract respiratory disease at a much higher rate than non athletes (reported in 1989 by Dr. Owen Anderson, editor of Running Research News published in Lansing Michigan).

b) athletes frequently complain of dry skin and blame it on weather or frequent showers.

c) we are experiencing a rash of "Chronic fatigue Syndrome" and "Fibromyalgia" cases particularly among female athletes.

and d) hemoglobin values seem difficult to maintain and can be related to low protein intake rather than low iron intake.

There is now considerable evidence that when the body is under physical or mental stress, the protein requirements go up. Under these stress conditions, the adrenal glands are stimulated to release cortisol (the body's natural form of cortisone).

Cortisol functions by removing nitrogen from protein molecules and rapidly turning protein to carbohydrate to maintain blood sugar levels in the brain. It is known as a "carbohydrate sparing" mechanism which is very active during prolonged submaximal exercise and during mental stress. If adequate protein (amino acids) is not circulating and available, the cortisol mechanisms will obtain the protein molecules from our body tissues. Because the cortisol is not fussy about which tissues it chooses, in extreme cases, we literally consumes ourselves to maintain that energy supply for the brain. We have all seen the individual who, under long term stress, physically deteriorates in size. This is the mechanism at work. Other less obvious examples could be just about any organ related illness because all organs are highly concentrated protein sources in the view of the hormone cortisol.

The third group experiencing PEM is the elderly !!

The third group experiencing PEM is the elderly. According to **Dr. William Evans**, formerly of Tufts University and now at Pennsylvania State University, in an article in American Health, March/April 1983, any person who eats only the minimum protein could find themselves protein deficient after a bout of moderate exercise or during a physically demanding job. It has been demonstrated that protein Calories can account for six to nine per cent (6 -9%) of total Caloric expenditure during exercise. That may not seem like much, but during a 10K (6 mile) run, I spend approximately nine hundred (900) Calories (according to the estimated calculation on the treadmill display console at my fitness club). If eight per cent (8%) of those Calories are from protein, it represents seventy-two (72) protein calories which is eighteen (18) grams of protein. That would be thirty per cent (30%) of my protein intake if I followed the RDA / RNI tables.

Once again, the RDA / RNI tables suggest the same level of protein intake for adults regardless of weight and physical activity habits. Such an assumption borders on stupidity. Protein requirements are unique for each individual and depend on physical activity, stress, genetic background and protein sources. The stress and physical activity portions of this equation has been discussed at length in a book by Leon Chaitow entitled "Amino Acids in Therapy" published in 1985. Chaitow

> **Protein requirements are unique for each individual !!**

observed that there is more to protein deficiency than just the oral supply. We must also consider the form of the ingestion (raw, cooked, vegetable, animal, etc.), the genetics of the individual and the food source, the digestibility, absorption which will be affected by other nutrients present or absent and the individual metabolism.

Dr. Roger Williams (discovered the B vitamin known as pantothenic acid) from the University of Texas published in his book **"Biochemical Individuality"** in 1956 that the individuality of amino acid concentration requirements may show the RDA / RNI to be low by a factor of three (3). This finding was supported by **Dr. Jeffery Bland** in the book **"Medical Application of Clinical Nutrition"** in 1983 where he indicated through experimental evidence that individual amino acid requirements differ by between two (2) and nine (9) fold. While on the same subject, **Dr. Vernon Young** of MIT Laboratory of Human Nutrition, School of Science presented research in the American Journal of Clinical Nutrition in 1989 which showed current protein recommendations to be low by a factor of two (2) to three (3) fold. He supported his findings with experimental radioactive labelled amino acid tracer protocol. Dr. Young is probably the most prominent protein research scientist in America.

Back in 1977 - 78, **Dr. Emanuel Cheraskin**, a former professor of Dentistry at the University of Alabama published

> **Those with the most symptoms consumed the least protein !!**

several studies to assess protein and / or amino acid requirements based on consumption and disease symptoms correlations. Upon assessing the symptoms (using the Cornell Medical Index Health Questionnaire) reported by 1040 dentists and their wives he learned that those reporting the most symptoms consumed the least protein. Conversely, those who consumed the most protein (2 -3 times the U.S RDA) displayed the fewest symptoms.

A Japanese paper by **Dr. Toshihiisa Matsuzaki** of the University of Ryukyus published in Nutrition Reviews, September, 1992 reported two interesting trends. First, between 1950 and 1983, the Japanese diet progressively increased **protein consumption from animal protein sources** up to approximately sixty-five (65) to seventy (70) grams per person day. At this peak, the correlation with life expectancy was at its best. Second, the animal protein consumption only accounted for half the Japanese protein intake. Therefore they must be consuming an average of one hundred and thirty to one hundred and forty (130 - 140) grams of total protein per person per day. This represents two (2) to three (3) times more than the recommended levels for North Americans. It is also true the Japanese are the largest consumers per capita of fish in

Early diets contained about 30% protein !!

the world and they also make liberal use of the soybean which is a good source of protein in addition to the protective phytochemical compounds known as isoflavones.

The North American diet pattern is lower in protein, approximately seventy (70) grams per person per day and sixty-five per cent (65%) from animal protein with a much lower ratio of fish than that found in the Japanese diet.

If we assume that the longer life expectancy of Japanese population is due to their diet and we wish to follow suit, the following change would be necessary. We would need to eat more:

    a) protein
    b) fish protein
    c) vegetable protein
    d) soy protein products.

According to **Dr. S Boyd Eaton**, an authority on prehistoric diets, in a paper published in to Journal of Nutrition in June of 1996, early diets contained about thirty per cent (30%) protein. Much of that protein was what people now call "game meat" which is leaner and higher in essential fatty acids. I would assume that the prehistoric population was following nature, unlike current diets which are dramatically controlled by manufacturing processes.

I need to briefly address the safety of increasing protein intake. One of the perpetuated myths about protein consumption is that high protein diets deplete calcium stores and lead to osteoporosis. The late **Dr. Carton Fredericks** provided an apt answer for those critics in his book **"Program for Living Longer"** I paraphrase with -'if high protein diets deplete calcium, we should have an Eskimo population devoid of bones. The Eskimo's (Inuit)consume and average of 265 to 300 grams of protein per day and yet neither life threatening coronary thrombosis nor osteoporosis appear to be to be a problem' .

The **Krogh's**, a husband -wife medical team studied Greenland Eskimos and found they consumed an average of 280 grams of protein per day. Apparently these people demonstrated excellent health and endurance and no evidence of osteoporosis, kidney disease nor liver disease. The explorers, referred to earlier in this book, Stefansson and Anderson, followed the high meat diet of

> **Stefansson and Anderson consumed 100 - 140 grams of protein / day !!**

the Eskimos for over one year while under hospital observation. During the year their average protein consumption was one hundred (100) to one hundred and forty (140) grams per day and two hundred (200) to three hundred (400) grams of fat daily. They demonstrated good health, no high blood pressure, and no liver nor kidney deterioration.

There is one study using exceptionally high protein intakes of six hundred (600) grams per day that showed undesirable kidney function resulting in excess calcium flushing in the urine. However, six hundred grams of protein per day represents eighty (80) to eighty-five (85) per cent of possible Calories which would be very unpalatable if not impossible to follow for long. Protein controls appetite and highly concentrated protein products are not very tasty. **Briggs and Calloway** wrote in **"Nutrition and Physical Fitness"** "...there is no indication of harm to healthy adults from consumption of 300 grams of protein daily if enough drinking water is available to take care of extra urinary wastes..."

Protein is the metabolic activator !!

Although, the **Better Balanced Diet** advocates an increase in protein consumption, it does not recommend three hundred (300) grams per day unless you are a very large high performance athlete.

Protein has been described as the **metabolic activator**. This single most important nutrient is indispensable to life because it is involved in every part of every cell function. In addition to its many attributes already discussed, it also forms muscles, hemoglobin, antibodies, chromosomes and DNA. The hemoglobin topic reminds me of some research by **Dr. Doug Clement** during the 1976 Olympic Games in Montreal. Dr. Clement studied one hundred and twenty three (123) male and sixty-four (64) female Canadian Olympic athletes and found they had significantly lower hemoglobin values than the Canadian general population. There score were also lower than the 1968 Australian Olympic team and the 1968 Dutch Olympic team. It was determined that this low hemoglobin level, which by the way is not good for an athlete attempting to deliver optimum oxygen to muscle cells, was due to **"suboptimal dietary intake of protein"**.

Three vital reasons why you need protein at optimal levels:

a) Protein drives the metabolic cycle known as catabolism / anabolism. Catabolism refers to the breakdown (burning - if you like) of tissue and anabolism is the reconstruction, building and repair phase of metabolism. Protein consumption stimulates the anabolism or **anabolic** phase which will help to increase or maintain "muscle tone". Following exercise, the catabolic phase, muscles require protein to stimulate the anabolic phase.

b) Protein drives the metabolic rate. After a meal, your metabolic rate (the rate at which you use Calories) increases due to the energy necessary to digest , absorb and assimilate the food components ingested. A

Protein drives the metabolic rate !!

high carbohydrate meal increases the metabolic rate by about four per cent (4%), whereas a high protein meal increases metabolic rate by twenty-five to thirty per cent (25 - 30%) and the increase lasts for up to twelve hours.

c) Protein consumption participates in the regulation of water balance. Just like certain minerals (potassium, sodium, calcium, magnesium, chloride and phosphorous) affect the osmotic control of water, so do protein molecules. When a diet is protein deficient, water will not be attracted to the proper vascular chambers, will not be excreted by the kidneys and result in peripheral accumulations known as edema or water retention. Thus one who is protein deficient will display puffy ankles and other signs of water retention.

The purpose of this chapter was to impress upon you the importance of protein and the consequences of Protein Energy Malnutrition. I also wanted to reassure you of the safety in more liberal protein consumption. Now that you understand these factors, why would ever take a chance of not consuming enough protein? The recommended levels of protein consumption in the **"Better Balanced Diet"**are outlined in the next chapter **"Lets Eat"**.

> **Remember, protein in every meal and every snack!!**

8

LET'S EAT !!

If you have diligently read every page of this book so far you are probably saying to yourself something like "alright already, when do we start eating"? The answer is "in a minute or two after we have set the ground rules designed to help you become successful with this method of food selection.

Any diet requiring precise measurements, radically restricted quantities, "weird food", special mixes and a great memory is doomed to failure. In this chapter there are some good menu choices with measurements included. However, this is not a cook book nor am

> **This not a cook book, nor am I a cook !!**

I a cook, so you are free to process the ingredients to your liking an to make "responsible substitutions". Go ahead and use the flavor enhancers, assuming they are safe, healthy and basically Calorie free or at least void of carbohydrates. Dr. Barry Sears recently published a book containing one hundred and fifty (150) recipes which are 40 - 30 - 30 favorable. "Zone Perfect Meals in Minutes" is the title. There are also some interesting recipes and ideas for a 40 - 30 - 30 diet on a Web site known as www.karenskitchen.com. (this site was available at press time but remember that web site addresses can change without notice). I included the contents of seven good breakfasts, seven good lunches, seven good dinners and a cross section of reasonable snacks which meet the criteria for the **Better Balanced Diet**. Before looking at your grocery list and menu suggestions, I discuss some other guidelines and rationale which should help you with your paradigm shift.

Eating is part of your lifestyle, acquired over the years. Lifestyle changes usually take some time and are maintained better if performed slowly, in small steps, over time. For many, a dramatic change, unless

> **those with serious health problems, should make radical changes quickly !!**

imposed by prescription and rigidly monitored, will be traumatic, stressful and result in poor compliance. Some people, those with serious health problems, should make a radical change quickly in the interest of developing better health as soon as possible. Professional advice from a knowledgeable nutrition oriented lifestyle consultant could be advisable if your health or body weight is seriously compromised (responsible and knowledgeable implies they have shifted their paradigm away from low Calorie - low fat thinking). Most readers of this material are experiencing the early signs of the SNAD diet and are willing to take charge on their own. I am referring to those who:

a) don't eat that much but still can't lose weight,

b) exercise regularly but still can't lose weight,

c) can't seem to get rid of

    i) the "spare tire" around the mid-section.

    ii) those "love handles" (casserole handles).

    iii) that "pot" (beer) - belly .

d) feel that they look like a pear with legs,

e) experience inflammation problems along with

    i) high blood pressure

    ii) elevated cholesterol

    iii) elevated triglycerides

or iv) hypoglycemia.

If you are one those, this chapter should help you make changes with relative ease and provide some degree of correction for the aforementioned problems.

    Better Balanced Dieting is not very restrictive and relatively easy to achieve compliance. In my previous work I had adopted the "food swap" phrase to identify a unit of measurement for the three macro nutrients; protein, carbohydrates and fats. The idea of **SWAP** was to signify some flexibility in choosing your food within guidelines. Other writings use words like servings, exchanges, blocks and units. When Dr. Sears developed the Zone Diet he popularized the unit known as the **Block**. Upon examining his Blocks, I learned that my Swaps used in my sports nutrition programs were almost the same, except a Swap of carbohydrate was 15 to 16 grams and a Block in the Sears program was 8 to 9 grams. To give you more flexibility in selecting food combinations which meet the 40 - 30 - 30 criteria, I have adjusted my Swaps to fall in line with Sear's Blocks.

    A Swap of :

    Protein = 7 grams

    Carbohydrate = 9 grams

and   **Fat = 3 grams when referring to an oil product or 1.5 grams when part of protein food like meat or fish and cheese.**

To maintain the 40 - 30 - 30 balance in any given meal or snack you should consume an equal number of Swaps for each of the three macro nutrients. This becomes an easy way to balance the diet. Merely become familiar with Swap sizes of the various foods or follow the table provided. Your alternative is to use a copy of something like the tables at the back of "Nutrition Almanac" or a computer data base to actually calculate your percentages of the various nutrients. Either way is acceptable.

PHASE I : the First Two Weeks

This period is called the **"Kick start"** or the **"Induction"** phase. Begin your change with eating five (5) small meals or three (3) meals and two (2) snacks each day. Remember - every meal and every snack must contain a good portion of protein (14 - 21 grams or 2 - 3 swaps - look at the Swaps chart for suitable choices and sizes). Be very conscious of and minimize or avoid the foods containing high glycemic index carbohydrates (If you are not sure of these foods, you may order a comprehensive list from the publisher - see back of book). These are likely the processed grains, pastas, food in boxes, sweet foods, breads, muffins, "comfort foods" and instant foods. Your local convenience store will not be a good source of groceries. Never have a glass of wine nor a bottle

> **Your local convenience store will not be a good source for groceries !!**

beer without some cheese or meat. Remember to avoid white bread, white sugar, white flour products and white rice or "puffed" rice and wheat products. Reduce or control bananas, carrots, raisins, white potatoes and other starchy foods because of their high GI.

If you are obese, requiring significant weight loss, you might try the Dr. Atkins "Induction phase" or the "Protein Power" program by the Eades or the "Endocrine Control Diet" by Ezrin for the first two weeks. These diet plans all restrict carbohydrate intake to twenty to forty (20-40) grams per day and are considered to be "Ketogenic"diets. Ketogenic diets are not dangerous and the American Dietetic Association has guidelines on how to manage Ketogenic diets. The **Better Balanced Diet** promoted in this book is **not Ketogenic**. I only suggest ketogenic diets for a short period of time for those considered obese and need a quick start program to show some results.

If you **Start your supplement program !!**
are not on a
responsible food supplement program, now is the time to
start. Re-read the chapter dealing with supplements and begin
using a basic program. You will be glad you started.

PHASE II: the Third Week

This should be your first true 40 - 30 - 30 week. I
suggest you try the following combination(s):

Two meals per day of a protein shake and meal
replacement bar (yes both). The total Calories, even though
we don't count Calories in this program, will be around five
hundred (500) or less per meal. The **protein powder** should
contain fourteen to sixteen (14 - 16) grams of soy protein
isolate (to get the benefits of the isoflavones in soy),
approximately eight to ten (8 - 10) grams of carbohydrate,
some of which should be fructose, one gram of fat and mixed
in water or 2% milk (8 oz.). **The bar** should also contain
twelve to fourteen (12 - 14) grams of protein, approximately
thirty (30) grams of carbohydrate and eight to ten (8 - 10)
grams of fat. (Yes I do have my favorite brand name for these
items) Be fussy about the type or source of fat in the bar. This
procedure is designed to help you feel the difference
immediately. I am talking about a difference in energy,
concentration and alertness. Remember that protein helps you
be alert, carbohydrates calm you and put you to sleep and
good fats help to metabolize the other fats.

For the evening meal try a stir- fry with wild rice and
your favorite protein source - beef, chicken, fish, or tofu (no
carrots, corn or potatoes).

For the evening meal try a stir- fry with wild rice and your favorite protein source - beef, chicken, fish, or tofu (no carrots, corn or potatoes).

For your choice of good snacks try one ounce of cheese or turkey or chicken and a fruit swap (see the table for swaps) or one cup of 1% milk and 4 almonds or ½ cup of plain yogurt.

You may stay with Phase II as long as you wish !!

If you are not already enjoying some fat burning physical activity regularly (3 or more times per week) , now is the time to start your exercise progarm.

You should now be ready to seriously start the paradigm shift to a 40 - 30 - 30 plan.

PHASE III : Fourth Week and from Now On!

After three weeks of "awareness" eating or induction dieting move toward the **Better Balanced Diet** suggested meals. These are not magic meals but rather simply meals containing the 40 - 30 - 30 balance. You could stay with Phase II for a very long time if you wish. After all Phase II is really easy to prepare and follow. However most people prefer more variety in their life and need to eat "regular meals". Responsible substitutions (that is why I use the word **Swaps** instead of blocks, servings, exchanges or units.)are fine or check out Dr. Barry Sears books on the Zone Diet or the Internet Web sites and some of its links, if you need more variety.

If you are serious, and I hope you are, you need to be sure your kitchen includes a good food scale (digital is best), measuring cups and spoons. Get serious about understanding quantities and sizes. After a couple of months experience your eyes, hands and fingers will be good measuring devices but they do need training.

You already know what four (4) ounces of hamburger or steak look like (¼ pounder). Buy a pound (454 grams for the Canadians) of cheese and cut it into sixteen (16) equal parts to visualize one ounce

Measure your milk, pasta, & cereal !!

of cheese (Please don't buy those processed slices - buy good 'real' cheese). Measure your milk, pasta, cereal, etc. until you have a "feel" for quantity.

Some of the steps I take when eating in restaurants are to a) never eat the bread or buns, b) only eat one slice or ½ the bun with a sandwich or burger and c) only eat ½ the potatoe or rice or pasta provided. At my favorite local restaurant I frequently attend "half-price pasta" night but I pay for them to double the meat or fish which I eat and I take home half the pasta and use it with some meat or fish in my own kitchen a few days later.

Your new lifestyle is part of your greater health plan, not a short term "fix-it" program. It is more than weight loss. This program is to help you control your basic metabolism by controlling the balance between the two major pancreatic hormones, insulin and glucagon.

It also helps to control the production of those very specialized but very transient hormone-like substances known as the eicosanoids. Remember the eicosanoids which are produced (if you are eating the right foods) as we need them and are not stored but move on in metabolism very quickly. The eicosanoids which include the prostaglandins were discussed briefly in the Insulin chapter. Eicosanoid production is dependent upon the correct balance and quantity of essential fatty acids (EFA's), the correct balance of insulin to glucagon and the quantity of saturated fat in the diet.

A Word About EFA's

A complete discussion on eicosanoids and EFA's would require another book but I feel a need to reinforce some of the concepts as you begin to select your foods. If you wish to read more about this I

GLA & EPA are precursors to the eicosanoids !!

recommend the book "Fats that Heal and Fats that Kill" by Udo Erasmus or "Good Fat, Bad Fat" by Loise Lambert-Lagace and Michelle LaFlamme or a new book "The Omega Plan" by Dr. Artemis Simopoulos.

The "super hormone" effectiveness of the eicosanoids requires the consumption of adequate levels of essential fatty acids in an appropriate ratio. Apparently, the ratio of Omega-6 to Omega-3 fatty acids found in nature is one to one (1:1) but in our current food supply it is closer to twenty to one (20:1). This imbalance may be responsible for many of the inflammatory conditions which are so prevalent today. Several researchers have suggested that for optimum health we need a ratio of three or four to one (3 or 4 : 1).

The EFA's, alpha linolenic acid (ALA) an Omega-3 and linoleic acid (LA) an Omega-6 or their activated versions eicosapentaenoic acid (EPA) and gamma linolenic acid (GLA) respectively, are precursors to all of the eicosanoids explained in brief in Chapter six.

How much of EFA's do we need? Erasmus suggests three to ten per cent (3 - 10%) of Calories should be EFA's. Translated into grams, that would represent nine to thirty

9 - 30) grams per day (10% of a 2,000 Calorie diet is 200 Calories which equals 22 - 23 grams). If the ratio of Omega-6 f Omega-3 were at three to one, it would mean consuming ighteen grams of Omega-6 and six grams of Omega-3 fatty cids per day. I would suggest that a good ortion of these EFA's

Take lecithin supplements !!

e derived from the activated versions, namely GLA and EPA, n view of the number people with metabolic imbalances vhich prevent the conversion of the simple oils to the activated orm (alpha linolenic acid to EPA and linoleic acid to GLA).

To obtain a reasonable balance in EFA's, use these guidelines:

a) Eat food rich in Omega-3 fatty acids, like salmon, trout, herring, mackerel, walnuts, flax seeds and green leafy vegetables:

b) Use predominately mono-unsaturated oils like extra virgin olive, sesame and peanut to reduce the formation arachidonic acid (the inflammatory fatty acid). There are others but usually harder to find;

c) Take lecithin supplements derived from the soy bean (use at least 2 grams = 4 capsules in a good product. Soy lecithin caps. are 56% Omega-6 and 9% Omega-3. Be very careful about quality. Never use un-capsuled lecithin oil nor lecithin granules- they are usually rancid due to exposure to air.);

d) use at least three (3) EPA capsules which should provide 500+ mg of this activated EFA;

e) use at least two (2) GLA capsules derived from borage oil which should provide approximately 180 mg of this activated EFA. If you use evening primrose capsules, you will need twice as many capsules;

f) conservative use of flax seed, pumpkin seed or walnut oil is suitable for cold oil applications as a means of increasing the EFA content of the diet;

g) become very conscious of 'trans-fatty' acid source and avoid them like you would avoid a bad disease

h) remember that although liberal use of Olive oil i recommended, it does not provide EFA's;

i) all oils should be cold pressed or at least expeller pressed to avoid the development of 'trans-fatty acid' accumulation. Tans-fatty acids are very damaging to healthy cells.

Comment on Protein Requirements

If you read Chapter 7 "Protein is the Answer" you know that I favor a protein intake equivalent to two to three (2 - 3) times greater than current RDA / RNI levels. This position is backed by sound scientific documentation and some experience. In the following guidelines, you begin selecting your diet by establishing your protein needs based on desirable weight and physical activity level.

> **I favor a protein intake equivalent to 2 - 3 time the RDA !!**

The other consideration if you plan to follow a 40 - 30 - 30 program is that the ratio of protein to carbohydrate should therefore ideally be 0.75. We have learned that a range of 0.65 to 0.95 would still keep you within reasonable limits.

GUIDE TO THE BETTER BALANCED DIET

The following will serve as a frame of reference to your new eating plan. You likely do not have a food science laboratory available to you, so all items and quantities are approximate because you will have to rely on your eyes and common sense during food selection.

1. Establish your protein requirements first.

This is very important. If you are:

a) Sedentary   0.75 x weight (lbs) = protein grams

b) Moderately active   1.00 x weight (lbs) = proteins grams

c) Aerobic Training   1.15 x weight (lbs) = protein grams

d) Intense Training   1.25 x weight (lbs) = protein grams

Divide your protein grams by 7 for the number of protein rich food swaps.

Weight refers to desirable weight.

If your are more than 20 % overweight, consider having your fat-free weight (lean body mass) assessed by your local fitness club or a personal consultant.
Then multiply Fat Free Weight (lbs.) (lean body mass in pounds) by 0.8, 1.20, 1.40, 1.60 respectively.

2. Plan to eat 5 - 6 times per day . Approximately every 3 hours.

3. No more than 6 Swaps of Protein rich choices per sitting. (approximately 40 grams of protein is the upper limit of absorption per meal)

4. Eat protein in every meal and every snack. Never eat Carbohydrates alone.

5. Every Meal and every snack should have an equal number of Protein, Carbohydrate and Fat Food Swaps.

Protein Swaps-selected from the 4th column of the "Food Swap Equivalent Tables", - average 7 gm (28 Calories),

Carbohydrate Swaps-Selected from the first 3 columns of the "Food Swap Equivalent Tables", - average 9 gm. (36 Calories) and Fat Swaps - selected from the 4th column & last cell of the "Food Swap Equivalent Tables", - average 3 gm. (27 Calories). If the Protein sources are higher fat, then Fat swaps should be 1.5 gm. (13.5 calories). This is designed to come close to a 40% carbohydrate, 30% protein, 30% good fat diet plan

6. Avoid or minimize eating high Glycemic Index Carbohydrates. That includes refined products like most grain flours, Breads, Cereals, Pasta, Cakes, Cookies, Rice and other starchy foods.

Do Not Eat: Corn, White Rice, Raisins, White Bread or Buns, most Bagels, Muffins, Doughnuts, Soda Pop - regular nor diet.

Restrict: Carrots, Parsnips, Beets, Bananas, White Potatoes, Breads, Dried Fruits and all Fruit Juices.

7. Be moderate in the consumption of animal fat (inflammatory Arachidonic Acid). Increase essential fats if you eat high animal fat or fried foods.

8. Fat choices should be from Essential Fatty Acid sources. Choose cold pressed or at least expeller pressed oils, nuts & seeds, avocados, olives, cold water fish like salmon, anchovies, mackerel and high quality supplements like lecithin, GLA, & EPA. (EPA : GLA ratio should be 3 : 1).

9. NEVER EAT deep fried grease, cheap oils or margarine of any kind.

10. NEVER heat fats and oils at high temperatures for more than 15 minutes. Heated oils turn to toxic trans-fatty acids.

11. Carbohydrates should come from higher fibre vegetables and fruits.

12. Eat as close to nature as possible. Organic will always be best. Avoid all unnecessary processing.

Before you jump into the seven suggested breakfasts, lunches and dinners you might like to look at the following grocery list. This grocery list includes all of the foods listed in the sample menus and should demonstrate to you that the food selection is quite "normal" and not exotic. Naturally you will need to add your own herbs and spices for seasoning to taste. The fruit and meat components of the list is long but you are free to "swap" choices according to the food swaps guide following the grocery list. That is why they are called "Swaps".

Grocery Shopping List

eggs	Crab meat
Cheddar Cheese	Shrimp
Yogurt - plain	Back (Canadian) bacon
Cottage cheese	Ground beef - lean
Butter	Ham
	Turkey
Strawberries	Chicken
Cantaloupe	Fish Fillets -unbreaded
Grapefruit	Pork chops -medium
Apricots	Corned beef
Apples	
Nectarines	Peanuts -unsalted
Oranges	Sunflower seeds - unsalted
Plums	Hazelnuts
Peaches	Almonds
Lemons	Macadamia nuts
Cranberries	Peanut butter -no salt-nor sugar
Pears	Real Mayonnaise
Raspberries	Olive oil - extra virgin
Grapes	White wine - dry
	Dijon mustard

Broccoli	Rye Bread - course
Asparagus	Oatmeal - Large Flake
Cauliflower	English Muffins - whole grain
Spinach	Mini pita pockets - whole grain
Green Peppers	
Potatoes - small	Protein Supplement - - 14 -16 gm protein / serving
Brussels sprouts	
Romaine Lettuce	Meal Replacement Bar - 13 - 15 gm protein / bar - 30 - 31 gm carbohydrate / bar
Onions	
Mushrooms	Rosemary
Celery	Tarragon
Zucchini	Dill
Kidney Beans	Cinnamon
	Nutmeg

SOME FOOD SWAP EQUIVALENTS	
FRUIT / Good !	**GRAINS / Not so Good !**
Apple ½	Bagel, English Muffin, Pita ¼
Applesauce ⅓ cup	Biscuit, Whole Wheat Bread, Blueberry Muffin, Hamburger Bun, Tortilla, Waffle, Doughnut Dinner Roll, 4" Pancake ½
Blueberries ½ cup	
Cherries ¾ cup	
Grapefruit, orange, Pear ½	Dry Cereal, Croutons, Melba Toast, Bread Crumbs, ½ oz.
Kiwi, Lemon, Lime 1	
Cantaloupe / Honeydew ¼	Breadstk,TacoShell,Rice Cake 1
Peach, Plum, Tangerine 1	Rice (brown or White) ckd, Pasta ckd Egg Noodles ¼ cup
Raspberries, Strawberries 1 C	
FRUIT / Not so Good !	**OTHER / Not so Good !**
Raisins 1 - 2 TBSP	Beer 6 oz
Juices: Tomato, V-8 1 cup Cranberry, Grape, Pineapple ¼ cup Apple, Grapefruit, Orange ⅓ cup	Wine 4 oz
	Spirits 1 oz
Banana ⅓ , Mango ⅓ cup,	Crackers 2 -4
Dates, Figs, Prunes 2 - 3 pieces	Ice Cream ¼ cup
Guava ½ cup, Papaya ¾ cup	Honey, Sugar, Molasses 2 tsp
GRAINS // Good	Tortilla or Potato Chips ½ oz
Barley(Pot) , Millet, Wild Rice, & Bulgur 1 TBSP (dry)	Barbeque, Plum,Oyster, Cocktail Teriyaki & Rum Sauces -2 TBSP
Oatmeal (Large Flake) ckd ⅓cup	Syrup , Maple 2 tsp
Rye Bread (Course) ½ slice	Candy Bar ¼

VEGETABLES-cooked // Good !	DAIRY & EGG // Good !	
Asparagus, Green or Wax Beans, Leeks, Sauerkraut, Turnip 1 cup	Milk 1% 1 cup	
	Yogurt - plain ½ cup	
Broccoli, Brussels Sprouts,Zucchini Cabbage, Eggplant, Squash, Spinach, Swiss Chard, 1½ cups	Cheese, Cottage Cheese ¼ cup Cheddar, Mozzarella, 1 oz Ricotta Cheese Skim 2½ oz	
Bok Choy, Cauliflower, 2 cups	Egg - Large 1	
Black Beans, Chick Peas, ¼ cup	MEATS ETC. // Good !	
VEGETABLES-raw // Good!	Beef or Game Grass Fed 1 oz	
Broccoli, Bamboo Shoots, 1½ Cups	Chicken, Turkey, Duck 1 oz	
Chopped onion, Snow Peas 1 cup	Back Bacon, Corned Beef 1 oz	
Cabbage, Cauliflower, Celery, Chopped Green Peppers 2 - 3 cups	Bass, Blue Fish, Lobster, Sardine, Trout, Tuna (in water) 1 oz	
Cucumber, Spinach, Mushrooms, Romaine Lettuce, chopped 4 cups	Catfish, Clams, Cod, Crab, Salmon , Halibut, Mackerel, Haddock 1½ oz	
Radish, Tomato (both sliced) 2 cups	Calamari (not breaded) 2½ oz	
Humus, Water Chestnuts ⅓ cup	Ham, Hamburger - lean 1½ oz	
VEGETABLES / Not so Good !	Lamb, Pork, Veal 1 oz	
Beans:Baked,Lima,Pinto,Refried¼c	MEAT ETC. / Not so Good !	
Squash - Acorn, Butternut ½ cup	Pepperoni, Salami, 1 oz	
Potatoes (all kinds) , Corn ¼ cup	Beef & Ground Beef fatty 1 oz	
Beets, Carrots, Parsnips ½ cup	Frankfurter (Beef, Pork,Turkey) 1	
Green Peas ⅓ cup	Liver (all varieties) 1 oz	

VEGETABLES (Protein Rich)	OTHER // Good !
Tofu (firm & Extra- Firm) 3 oz	3 Olives / Nuts & Seeds 1 TBSP or 6 Peanuts, 1 Macadamia nut,
Soy Burgers ½ Patty	Nut Butters, Tahini ½ tsp
Soy-hot dog, sausage,2 links/ 1patty	Cold Pressed Oils ⅓ teaspoon

NOTE -- the "not so good" items simply suggests that you should be cautious about how many swaps of that item you choose on any given day. It should not be construed as a "do not eat" warning.

SEVEN SAMPLE BETTER BALANCED DIET BREAKFASTS   (3 Swaps of Each)

PROTEIN	CARBOHYDRATE	FAT
Scrambled Eggs		
2 eggs 1 oz Cheese- Shredded	Fruit Swap ½ piece Rye Toast	⅔ tsp Olive Oil ½ tsp Peanut butter -no sugar
Oatmeal & Yogurt		
2 TBS Protein Powder, ½C Yogurt - Plain	⅓ C Oatmeal cooked nutmeg,,cinnamon	1 TBSP Almonds- slivered
Instructions: Add Protein Powder & Yogurt to cooked Oatmeal, top with Almonds.		
Fruit Salad		
¾ cup Cottage Cheese	1 C Strawberries ¾ C cantaloupe ½ C grapes	1 TBSP Almonds-slvrd
Yogurt & Fruit + Back Bacon		
1 C Yogurt Plain 1 oz Back Bacon	1 C Strawberries or ½ cup Blueberries or 1 sliced Peach 1 cup Raspberries	1 TBSP Almonds- slivered
Instructions: Mix together , top with Almonds. Cook Bacon separately		
French Toast		
2 Eggs ½ C Yogurt -Plain	Whole Grain Bread 1 slice 1 C Strawberries	1 TBSP Almonds slivered
Instructions: Beat Eggs, Soak 1 slice Bread-cook - add Strawberries, Yogurt & Almonds. Cook & eat any surplus Egg.		

PROTEIN	CARBOHYDRATE	FAT
Hash		
3 oz cooked meat	⅓C cked Potato 1C Tomato, Vegetables, ¼ Cantaloupe	1 tsp Olive or Sesame Oil
Instructions: Saute Vegetables in Oil , add Meat , Potatoes, Tomatoes, spices to choice. Cantaloupe is a side dish		
Eggs Benedict		
1 oz Back Bacon 2 Eggs	½ English Muffin ½ Grapefruit	1 TBSP Olive or Sesame Oil
Instructions: Poach Eggs, Cook Bacon, Toast Muffin, add Oil, stack		

SEVEN SAMPLE BETTER BALANCED DIET BREAKFASTS (6 swaps of Each)		
PROTEIN	CARBOHYDRATE	FAT
Scrambled Eggs		
4 eggs 1oz Cheese-Shred 1oz Back Bacon	1 Cantaloupe or 2 Peaches or 2 Cups Blueberries 1 piece Rye Toast	3TBSP Olive Oil, 1½ tsp Peanut butter
Oatmeal & Yogurt		
4 TBS Protein Pwdr (21 grams protein) 1 C Yogurt -Plain	1⅓ C Oatmeal dry, nutmeg, cinnamon, ½ Cantaloupe or 1 cup Raspberries	4 TBSP Almonds- slivered
Instructions: Add Protein Powder to cooked Oatmeal, top with Almonds. Cantaloupe as a side dish or Raspberries on top.		

PROTEIN	CARBOHYDRATE	FAT
Fruit Salad		
1½ cup Cottage Cheese	1 C Strawberries 1 C Melon ½ C Mandarins	12 Macadamia Nuts
Instructions: Mix together		
Yogurt & Fruit + Back Bacon		
1½C Yogurt Plain 3 oz Back Bacon	1½ C Pineapple or 2 cups of Blueberries	4 TBSP Almonds slvd
Instructions: Mix together, top with Almonds. Cook Bacon Separately.		
French Toast		
4 Eggs 2 oz Back Bacon	2 slices Whole Grain Bread, 2 C Strawberries /Raspberries	4 TBSP Almonds slvd
Instructions: Beat Eggs, Soak 2 slices Bread-cook -Top with Strawberries / raspberries & Almonds. Cook & Eat any surplus Egg.		
Hash		
6 oz cooked lean meat. (Chicken, ham, beef, etc.)	⅓ C cooked Potato 2 C Tomato, Vegetables ½ Cantaloupe or 2 Peaches	4 TBS Olive or Sesame or Walnut Oil
Instructions: Saute Vegetables, add Meat, Potatoes, Vegetables ,Spices		
Eggs Benedict		
2 oz Back Bacon 4 Eggs	1 English Muffin ½ Grapefruit 1CStrawberries	tsp Oil
Instruction: Poach Eggs, Cook Bacon, Toast Muffin, Add Oil, Stack		

SEVEN SAMPLE BETTER BALANCED DIET LUNCHES (3 Swaps of Each)		
PROTEIN	**CARBOHYDRATE**	**FAT**
Seafood Sandwich		
4½ oz crab, shrimp etc.	1 Apple, or 1 Pear , sml side salad,½ mini pita	1 TBS Mayo
Instructions: Mix Seafood with Mayonnaise Stuff into mini Pita Pocket		
Cheeseburger		
4½oz Hamburger 1 oz Cheese	Rye Bread 1 slice Tomato, Lettuce , 1 Kiwi	6 Peanuts
Chef Salad		
1½ oz ham 1½ oz turkey 1 oz Cheese	Large Tossed Green Salad 1 Nectarine or 1 Peach or 1 Cup Raspberries	1 TBS Oil & Vinegar Dressing
Chicken Salad		
3 oz Grilled Chicken	2 C Lettuce, ¼ C each of Onions, Mushrooms, Tomatoes, spices, 1 Orange	1 TBS Oil & Vinegar Dressing
Instructions: Prepare Salad, add dressing, Add lemon Juice, garlic, Worcestershire sauce,pepper. Top with Chicken, sprinkle Parmesan.		
Salmon Salad Sandwich		
4 oz Canned Salmon	Chopped Celery, onions to taste ½ C Blueberries,Lettuce, Tomato, 1slice Rye Bread	1 TBS Mayo
Instructions: Mix Salmon with Mayonnaise, onions, Lettuce, celery.		
Back Bacon Sandwich		
2oz Back Bacon 1 oz cheddar cheese	¼ Cantaloupe, 1 slice rye bread, Lettuce , Tomato	1 tsp Mayo 6 Olives

PROTEIN	CARBOHYDRATE	FAT
Turkey Pita		
3 - 4 oz Turkey	1 Mini Pita Pkt. ½ Green Pepper chopped , 1 Peach	1½ TBS Guacamole

SEVEN SAMPLE BETTER BALANCED DIET LUNCHES (6 Swaps of Each)		
PROTEIN	CARBOHYDRATE	FAT
Seafood Sandwich		
9 oz crab shrimp, Lobster, or Scallops	1 Orange, sml side salad, ½ pita pocket	2 TBS Mayo 2 TBS Oil & Vinegar Drsng
Cheeseburger		
7½oz Hamburger 1 oz Cheese	2 slices Rye Bread Tomato, Lettuce 1 Apple or 1 cup apple sauce	12 Macadamia Nuts
Chef Salad		
3 oz ham,+ 3 oz turkey, &2 oz Cheese	Large Tossed Green Salad 2 Nectarines or 2 Peaches	4 TBS Oil & Vinegar Dressing
Chicken Salad		
6 oz Grilled Chicken	3 C Lettuce, 1 C each of Onions, Mushrooms, 2 C Tomatoes, 1 Apple & 1 Pear	4 TBS Oil & Vinegar Dressing

Instructions: Prepare Salad, Add dressing, Add lemon juice, garlic, Worcestershire sauce, pepper. Top with Chicken, sprinkle Parmesan.

PROTEIN	CARBOHYDRATE	FAT
Salmon Salad Sandwich		
8 oz Salmon	Celery, Lettuce, 1 C Grapes, Tomato, 2 slices Rye Bread	4 TBS Mayo
Instructions: Mix Salmon with Mayonnaise, Lettuce, celery, & grapes		
Back Bacon Sandwich		
3oz Back Bacon 1½ oz Turkey & 1oz cheese	1 Peach, Tossed Salad, 2 slices rye bread, Lettuce , Tomato	1 TBS Mayo 3 TBS Olive Oil & Vinegar Drsng
Turkey Pita		
6 -9 oz Turkey	1 Pita Pocket, 1 Orange, Tomato, 1 Green Pepper & 1 Cup Strawberries	6 TBS Guacamole

SEVEN SAMPLE BETTER BALANCED DIET DINNERS (3 Swaps Each)		
PROTEIN	**CARBOHYDRATE**	**FAT**
Chili		
4½ oz Lean Ground Meat & ½ oz shredded cheddar cheese	Onion, Grn Peppers Mushrooms, spices ¼ C Kidney Beans 1 C Tomatoes, 1 Kiwi	1 tsp Olive or Sesame or Walnut Oil
Instructions: Brown meat in oil @vegetables &spices, Add beans & tomatoes simmer 30 min. Top with shredded cheese.		

PROTEIN	CARBOHYDRATE	FAT
Baked Chicken		
3 oz Chicken Breast - skinless	1¼C Broccoli Steamed, Spinach Salad, Lemon & Onion slices ¼ Cantaloupe	1 TBS Oil
Instructions: Bake Chicken covered with lemon & onion @ 450°F 15 min., reduce heat to 350°F season of choice & cook 10 -15 min.		
Fish		
4½ oz Fish Fillets, ½ oz shredded cheese	1 C Spinach chopped Salad, Onion, Pepper, Lemon juice ½ Pear	1 TBS Oil & Vinegar Dressing
Instructions: Wrap Fish , onion, pepper, lemon juice, & cheese in oil sprayed foil. Bake at 425°F 18 min.		
Pork Chops & Green Salad		
2 average pork chops	½ Apple slcd,¼Cwater 1Tbs White Wine, Dijon Ms 1½C Cauliflower stmd, Rosemary	1 TBS Oil & Vinegar dressing
Instructions: Top Pork @apple, rosemary, & mustard in baking dish. Pour in wine & water , bake @ 450°F 15 min. Baste Pork @ juices, reduce heat to 350°F 10 - 15 min.		
Meatloaf		
4½ oz Ground Beef (lean) & 1 Egg	¼ C Onions, Bread Crumbs Pepper, 1½ C cooked Zucchini, ½ Apple, & a tossed salad	1 TBS Oil & Vinegar dressing
Instructions: Mix Meat, egg, ketchup, onions, bread crumbs, pepper & Worcestershire sauce in loaf dish, microwave 10 - 15 min on medium or 'til done.		

PROTEIN	CARBOHYDRATE	FAT
Roast Turkey		
4½ oz Turkey Breast	1½ C steamed Brussels Sprouts, ½ C onions - boiled ½ C Cranberries	1 TBS Almonds - slivered
Baked Fish		
4½ oz Fish Fillet	1 ½C Asparagus cooked, Lemon 2 Tomatoes broiled Rosemary, Tarragon, Dill, & ½ Pear	1 tsp Olive Oil
Instructions: Rub or cover Fillet with Herbs & Oil ,Bake 10-15 min., Garnish with lemon.		

SEVEN SAMPLE BETTER BALANCED DIET DINNERS (6 Swaps Each)		
PROTEIN	CARBOHYDRATE	FAT
Chili		
7½ oz Lean Ground Meat 1 oz shrd cheese	Onion, Grn Peppers Mushrooms spices , ¾C Kidney Beans 1 C Tomatoes, & 2 Peaches	4 tsp Oil
Instructions: Brown meat in oil @vegetables &spices, Add beans & tomatoes simmer 30 min. Top with shredded cheese.		
Baked Chicken		
6 oz Chicken Breast - skinless	1½ C Broccoli steamed, Spinach Salad, Lemon & Onion slices , 1 c Strawberries & 1 Apple	4 TBS Oil
Instructions: Bake Chicken covered with lemon & onion @ 450°F 15 min., reduce heat to 350°F add spices of choice & cook 10 -15 min.		

PROTEIN	CARBOHYDRATE	FAT
Baked Fish		
9 oz Fish Fillets ½ oz shredded cheese	2 C Spinach, ½ C Pasta cooked, Tossed Salad, Onion, Pepper, Lemon , 4 Apricots	4 TBS Oil & Vinegar Dressing
Instructions: Wrap Fish , onion, pepper, lemon juice, & cheese in oil sprayed foil. Bake at 425°F 18 min.		
Baked Pork Chops & Spinach Salad		
3 pork chops	1 Apple slcd,1Tbs WhiteWine, ¼C water, Rosemary, DijonMst 1½C stmd Cauliflower, 1Peach	4 TBS Oil & Vinegar dressing
Instructions: Top Pork @apple, rosemary, & mustard Pour in wine & water , bake @ 450°F 15 min. Baste Pork @ juices, reduce heat to 350°F 10 - 15 min.		
Meatloaf		
9 oz Ground Beef or Turkey - lean , 1 Egg	¼ C Onions, Bread Crumbs Pepper, 1½ C cooked Zucchini 1 Apple, 1 Orange, tossed salad	4 TBS Oil & Vinegar dressing
Instructions: Mix Meat, egg, ketchup,onions,bread crumbs, pepper & Worcestershire sauce in loaf dish, microwave 10 - 15 min on medium		
Turkey Dinner		
9 oz Turkey Breast	3 C Brussels Sprouts, ½ C onions - boiled ½ C Cranberries, 1 Nectarine	1 TBS slivered Almonds + 9 Macadamia nts
Baked Salmon		
9 oz Salmon Fillet	1½ C Asparagus cooked. 2 brld Tomatoes, Rosemary,Tarragon, Dill, Lemon , 1 Apple + 1 Pear	1 tsp Oil
Instructions: Rub or cover Fillet with Herbs & Oil , Bake 10-15 min., Garnish with lemon..		

GOOD SNACKS (approximately 1 Swap for each item)
approximately 90 - 100 Calories per snack

1 oz. Cheese -low fat & ½ Orange	1 oz Back Bacon (cooked) & 1 cup V-8 Juice
1 oz Turkey & 1 Cup Strawberries & 6 Peanuts	1 oz Cheese - low fat + 1 Peach & 3 Olives
2½ oz Calamari + 1¼ Cups chopped Tomato & 1 TBS Sesame seed Oil	1 TBS Protein Powder + ½ Cup 1% Milk or 2 TBS Protein Powder in water.
⅓ Cup Oatmeal -cooked + 1 TBS Protein Powder & ½ cup 1% milk	½ Cup plain yogurt
¼ Cup Cottage Cheese low fat & ½ Cup diced Pineapple	1 oz Ham + ½ cup Honeydew Melon & 4 Pecans
1 oz Cheddar Cheese & ½ Apple	6 oz Beer + 1 oz Corned Beef
1 oz Turkey + ½ Cup Grapes & 1 Macadamia nut	1 oz slice cold beef - lean & ½ Pear
1 oz soft Cheese & 4 oz Wine	1 oz Tuna & 2 Kiwi fruit
½ TBS Guacamole + 1 oz sliced Turkey & ½ Cup Grapes	1½ oz Crab meat + ½ slice Rye Bread & ⅓ tsp Mayonnaise
1 oz Ham sliced + 1 Cup Strawberries & 3 Almonds	½ Cup Plain Yogurt & 2 tsp Sunflower seeds
2 oz Cottage Cheese - low fat + ¾ Cup Cantaloupe - cubed & 1 tsp Almonds slivered	½ slice course Rye Bread + ½ tsp natural Peanut Butter & 1 tsp Protein Powder
1 oz Chicken + 1 Cup Strawberries & 3 Olives	1 Cup 1% Milk + 4 Almonds
1 Hard Boiled Egg + ½ Apple & ½ tsp Peanut Butter on celery	⅓ Cup Oatmeal -cooked +1 TBS Protein Powder + ½ C 1% milk
1 oz Corned Beef + 1 Cup Raspberries & ½ TBS Guacamole	1½ oz Shrimp -cooked + 3 Apricots & 3 Hazelnuts

FOOD SWAP SYSTEM SUMMARY

Food Type	serving size	calorie count	protein gm.	carbs gm.	fat gm.
FRUIT					
Good	½C	30 - 40	0	7 - 10	0
Not so Good	¼-½ C	30 - 40	0	7 - 10	0
VEGETABLES					
Good cooked	1 cup	25 - 50	2 -4	7 - 10	0
Not so Good raw	1 - 2½ C	25 - 50	1½ - 3	7 -10	0
Not so Good cooked	¼ - ½ C	20 - 40	1 - 1½	7 - 12	0
Legumes cooked	¼ - ⅓ C	30 - 60	3 - 5	7 - 15	0
GRAINS					
Good cooked	⅓ C	40 - 60	3 - 5	8 - 12	1
Not so Good	¼ C	30 - 40	2 - 4	6 - 9	1
MILK & CHEESE PRODUCTS					
Good	½ - 1 C // 1 oz	100 - 150	7 - 9	.5 - 11	2 - 9
MEATS, POULTRY, FISH					
Good	1 - 1½ oz	50 - 80	6 - 8	0	4 - 8
Not so Good	1 oz	50 - 90	3 - 7	0	5 - 8

Food Type	serving size	calorie count	protein gm.	carbs gm.	fat gm.

OTHER ITEMS

Food Type	serving size	calorie count	protein gm.	carbs gm.	fat gm.
FATS	½ tsp	21	0	0	2.4
NUTS & SEEDS	1 TBSP	50	1 - 1.5	1 - 3	4 - 6
SUGARS	2 tsp	40	0	10	0

If you choose to design your eating plans through the grams and per cent methods the following calculator guide may be of help. Merely insert the data for each food item(s) under the appropriate columns and total each column. The arrows under the Calories total indicate the you should divide each Calorie column total by the total Calories and multiply by 100 to obtain per cent.

Although you objective is to come as close to 40 - 30 - 30 as possible, please do not become distraught over a few points or decimal places. The human body is not so precise that a few percentage points either way will make a big difference. 29 - 42 - 29 or 28 - 42 - 30 or 28 - 44 - 28 are all OK. Just don't stray too far from the ideal.

BETTER BALANCED DIET CALCULATOR

ITEM	Calories	Protein gm x 4 = Cal.		Carbohydrates gm x 4 = Cal		Fat gm x 9 = Cal	
1							
2							
3							
4							
5							
6							
Totals							
	↪ →→→→→ ÷			÷		÷	
			× 100	×	100	×	100
			%		%		%

_____ ÷ _____ = _____   (ideal = 0.75,

Protein grams   Carbohydrate grams   OK between 0.65 & 0.95)

If you prefer to use the Swap estimation method of designing your eating plan then the following chart may be of help. Remember that you should have the same number of Swaps for each of the macro nutrients in every meal and every snack and the maximum number of protein Swaps per meal or snack is six (6). If you are heavier or more active you will need to create another column or two for more meals and snacks.

MEAL PLANNING CHART FOR ONE DAY
_____ Swaps / day

Nutrient	Breakfast	Lunch	Snack	Dinner	Snack
Protein					
Protein					
Protein					
Protein					
Protein					
Protein					
Carbos					
Carbos					
Carbos					
Carbos					
Carbos					
Carbos					
Fat					
Fat					
Fat					
Fat					
Fat					
Fat					

An example using the first breakfast, lunch and dinner in the seven examples offered earlier in this chapter!

MEAL PLANNING CHART FOR ONE DAY
___11___ Swaps / day

Nutrient	Breakfast	Lunch	Snack	Dinner	Snack
Protein	1 Egg	1½ oz crab	1 oz Ham	1½ oz Ground beef	½Cup Yogurt
Protein	1 Egg	1½oz crab		1½ oz Ground beef	
Protein	1 oz Cheese	1½oz crab		1 oz Cheese	
Protein					
Protein					
Protein					
Carbos	½ Grapefruit	½ Apple	1 Cup Straw-berrys	¼ Cup Kidney beans	from yogurt
Carbos	½ Grapefruit	½ Apple		1¼ Cup Tomato	
Carbos	½ piece Rye Toast	½ mini Pita		1 Peach	
Carbos					
Carbos					
Carbos					
Fat	⅓tsp Olive oil	1 tsp Mayo	6 Pea-nuts	1 tsp Olive oil	2 tsp Sun flow-er seeds

Fat	⅓tsp Olive oil	1 tsp Mayo		balance from meat & cheese	
Fat	½tsp Peanut butter	1 tsp Mayo			
Fat					
Fat					

9

THE STUFF YOU ARE NOT EATING

To supplement or not to supplement? - that is the question - to be addressed by this chapter. After thirty-five (35) years in the wellness industry I am convinced that to maintain optimal health, supplementation is no longer an option. In fact that is the title of one of Dr. Bruce Miller's many nutrition booklets published from his offices in Dallas Texas. Dr. Miller outlines a very convincing case

Supplementation is no longer an option !!

for why supplementation has become a necessity if you wish to develop or maintain optimal health. This chapter is my version of the same argument. -There - I stated my position! The remainder is a discussion about why that is my position.

I, like most health professionals, was taught (some people say educated) that supplements were unnecessary and only created expensive urine (I am not sure who tested or sold this urine to determine it's value). The conventional wisdom was, and still is in many circles, that you could get all the nutrients you needed from a "well balanced diet". Sound familiar? However, about twenty-five (25) years ago, after some open minded reading and listening, I tried some supplements and was impressed with the results. This carried forward to my children, who had some health problems, and again we were impressed with the changes that took place in our lives. The testimonials of our successes are beyond the scope of this book but I needed to tell you that there are testimonials which, supported by science, changed my paradigm about supplementation.

Supplementation

Supplementation is**"No longer an option"** if optimal health is the objective. In fact, if you are not prepared to supplement your diet at some responsible level, I would question your sincerity in your desire to develop optimal health.

Such a dogmatic statement may seem unusual, but I have seen enough cases of people who have tried it both ways and I can assure the supplemented group always wins. It will undoubtedly require a paradigm shift for many of you, consumers and health professionals alike. We have been indoctrinated with the concept that "all you need is a well balanced diet"!! This may well be true, but the difficulty with accepting such a truth is two fold. First - which balance do you accept as ideal?

> **Where do you obtain the food, guaranteed to contain the nutrients recommended ??**

Second - where do you obtain the food, guaranteed to contain the nutrients recommended?   A third difficulty lies in the question - do you accept the "Recommended Daily Allowance (RDA's), Reference Daily Intakes (RDI's), Daily Values (DV's), Recommended Nutrient Intake (RNI's in Canada) as adequate for everyone and obtainable?

During recent years an increasing number of authoritative writers and scientists have broken with tradition and published research and commentary supporting the use of responsible supplementation

A study published in the Journal of the American Dietetic Association in 1984 by Dr. B. Worthington-Roberts entitled "Supplementation Patterns of Washington State Dieticians", demonstrated that sixty per cent (60%) of Registered Dieticians supplemented their diets. Now that was thirteen

"Supplementation Patterns of Washington State Dieticians"!!

years ago and I am certain that the number today is much higher when you consider the growth of the food supplement industry over the last five years.

Food supplement spending in North America has more than tripled in the last five years, now exceeding five billion dollars annually. Although that may sound like a lot of money until you divide it by the 290 million people in North America. That averages out to $17.24 per person per year. We have 1 long way to go before spending on food supplements reaches main stream levels.

Consider this, we (North Americans) spend annually: six billion dollars on cat food, nine billion dollars on dog food, eleven billion dollars on potatoe chips and 434 billion dollars on toys. Does this put it into perspective for you??

Since the publication of preliminary data from the ongoing Harvard Physicians' Health Study, a growing number of physicians have commenced with at least anti-oxidant supplementation. However, many are still resistant to the idea.

I find the health professional reluctance toward supplementation interesting and yet there are over six hundred (600) reported studies on vitamin C cited in the scientific literature with an overwhelming conclusion indicating numerous benefits. At least somebody considers the topic worth investigating. I wonder how long it will take before the results are accepted and incorporated into routine dietary recommendations?

Fundamentally, the rationale for food supplementation is one of relatively simple arithmetic. (Although not all simple arithmetic serves nutrition advice well, this example does simplify the facts.) We eat less than one half the Calories eaten by our ancestors in 1900. Further, throughout the

> ## We eat less than ½ the Calories eaten by our ancestors in 1900 !!

nutrition literature, it has been clearly demonstrated that if you reduce your Caloric intake it does not mean that you can afford a corresponding reduction in nutrients. Therefore, to obtain all the nutrients of a high Calorie diet on fewer Calories, you must eat food with a higher nutritional density (i.e. more vitamins etc. per Calorie). Do you believe, in this modern world of fast food, food technology and food processing, that this can and does occur? The answer is a simple no! If anything is true, the modern processed food is less dense in nutrients than the original non-processed food of the early 1900's.

Several studies have demonstrated that organically grown vegetables contain significantly more minerals than current conventionally grown produce in the presence of commercial fertilizers. I am talking about a three (3) to one hundred (100) times differential when I say "significant". (Ref. reported in Boode-Peterson, Tom H. "Energy News Updates, Project 2000 Inc. 140 Seawall Street, Boylston, Ma. Fall 1993, and by Firmma E. Beer Report, Rutgers University, Firmament Farming Magazine, 1991.) Just to offer you an example, the magnesium content of organic tomatoes was thirteen (13) times greater than that found in conventionally grown tomatoes and the copper content of organic cabbage was one hundred and twelve (112) times greater than that found in conventionally grown cabbage.

It has been reported that although commercially grown produce appears to yield more, it actually contains less dry matter after dehydration than the organically grown versions. The Object lesson here is apparent. In the late

> **In the late 1800's and early 1900's all produce was grown organically !!**

1800's - early 1900's all produce was organically grown. So, not only did our ancestors eat more (out of necessity), the nutritional content per Calorie of the food was higher.

Do not be fooled by the expression - "a tomatoe is a tomatoe is a tomatoe". I have heard anti-supplement Dieticians use this one many times. They contend that the tomatoe grows its nutrients for itself, not for you and if the tomatoe was low in nutrients, it would be very small, not grow well and the farmer would go bankrupt. Please, please, please understand that there are many varieties of every vegetable and that artificial fertilization can enhance one part of the plant but not necessarily the whole spectrum. Just as human beings can look similar and yet have varying degrees of bone density, fat content and muscle content, so can vegetables and other food products vary in nutrient content. The whole purpose of crop grading systems to reflect quality differences should speak volumes here. Grades for milling wheat are an excellent example. In Western Canada, grain farmers receive a premium price if they produce thirteen per cent (13%) protein wheat. This is the wheat which produces the best bread. However, only a small percentage of the wheat will meet these criteria. That should show you there are differences in the quality of produce you buy which go well beyond the obvious criteria of color appearance and size.

Nutrient loss following harvest is also a significant issue. The Berkeley Wellness letter in October of 1995 pointed out that if fresh produce is labeled for nutritional content, it is not measured but assumed to be at the levels stated in conventional textbooks. An item in the New York Times in the same year reported the actual vitamin C content in fourteen (14) packaged food items was eighty per cent (80%) less than that stated on the label. It has been estimated that fruits and vegetables lose up to eighty per cent (80%) of their nutrients within seventy-two (72) hours after harvesting. The report

45% of the population eat no fruit !!

showed a range of thirty per cent (30%) loss in strawberries to an eighty per cent (80%) loss in broccoli. Consequently the quality of the food you eat is not only dependent upon growing methods but also harvesting and processing. If you assume that textbook values of nutrients actually exist in all you eat, you may be leaving yourself at risk.

Another "reality check" deals with - what do you actually eat? A study published in the American Journal of Public Health in 1990 reported that forty-five per cent (45%) of the population eat no fruit nor fruit juice and forty-eight per cent (48%) ate no vegetables other than french fries. The Calgary Herald reported in October of 1992 that according to Statistics Canada, the potatoe has become the number one vegetable eaten. However, this includes the french fries and the potatoe chips. Consistent with the theme of this book, which is to control the glycemic index (starchy) carbohydrate intake, we find that the number one vegetable is the potatoe with a GI of 80 - 121 depending on how it is prepared. The number one fruit is the banana with a GI of 77 to 80 (very high).

If you are interested in other gory details about how poor our diet is you may like Dr. Bruce Millers booklet "Food Supplementation No Longer an Option" published in 1996. He reviews numerous interesting facts and figures, ranging from the power of the advertising dollar, food consumption patterns and the poor health consequences associated with these poor choices.

I am also asking you to pay particular attention to the meaning of the word supplementation. It means "to **supplement**", something extra or in addition to. My Random House dictionary defines supplement as "something added to complete a thing or supply a deficiency". It **does not** mean **Substitution**. Therefore you should select as good a diet as possible and complete it with responsible supplementation.

Many supplement advocates suggest there are three levels of supplementation. The first and most obvious is the level necessary to create a complete diet for you - as the above definition describes. The second level is one of protection. Your needs

> **Pay particular attention to the meaning of the word supplementation !!**

may vary depending on your life-style choices and the environment in which you live. The third level is that of therapy. Once symptoms of disease have made their presence known you may use extra nutrition in a therapeutic way. Frequently the mistake made here is to stop the supplementation after the symptoms have subsided as you might do with a conventional drug prescription. In nutrition you should simply adjust to a preventive or some call it a maintenance level which may in fact become part of your "complete diet ".

Returning to the arithmetic I referred to in the beginning of this chapter, I want to offer a few pertinent examples to punctuate the issue of necessary supplementation.

Supplementation for protection or prevention is where the arithmetic part of this equation becomes so important. In recent years numerous studies have been published by prestigious professionals in prestigious journals which

Supplementation for protection !!

lead us to the conclusions that the **daily protective levels of**:

> Vitamin A
>   (and/or Beta Carotene) exceed 30,000 IU (18 mg)
>   Vitamin E   exceeds   400 IU
>   Vitamin C   exceeds   1,000 mg
> and   Calcium   exceeds   1,000 mg

The first three are the major antioxidants which help to prevent free radical damage. Free radical damage is likely the most obvious cause of degeneration of cells leading to the major immune deficiency diseases including heart disease and cancer.

Carrots are a good source of beta carotene but you must eat at least four medium carrots **every day** to obtain 30,000 IU. Sweet potatoes are also a good source but you need three every day to match the protective level. Fresh tomatoes or cantaloupe also provide good levels of beta carotene but you would require one and one half (1½) cantaloupe every day to meet the minimal protective standards. I emphasize here the **minimal** protective standards as published by the ever cautious conservative university and medical science world.

Dr. Shari Lieberman, a Registered Dietician, published in the most recent edition of her book, "The Real Vitamin & Mineral Book", that the protective level of beta carotene could be up to **50,000 IU (30 mg)** per day (6 ½ carrots or 5 ½ sweet potatoes). Further support for supplemental beta carotene comes from two studies which compared carotenoid absorption from fresh vegetables to the absorption from high quality purified beta carotene capsules. In every case the supplemented trials demonstrated two to five times better absorption than the fresh vegetable trials in the subjects. (see references Brown, E.D. 1989 and Jensen, C.D. 1985). So it becomes apparent, with North Americans dismal vegetable consumption record, that the likelihood of eating at a protective level is very remote and supplementation is not an option for optimal health.

> **the protective level of beta carotene could be up to 50,000 IU (30 mg) per day !!**

The major sources of Vitamin E are selected nuts, oils, and grains. The following list clearly demonstrates the futility of attempting to obtain enough vitamin E from the diet. Your choices are obvious, try one of the following or a single concentrated 400 IU capsule. The vitamin E capsule should contain all eight forms of the vitamin (known as mixed tocopherols and tocientrols) and selenium which is a co-factor to vitamin E. Again Shari Lieberman's book describes the "optimal daily intake" as between 400 and 1200 IU per day (1 - 3 capsules).

VITAMIN E SOURCES & CONCENTRATIONS		
Food Item	**Vitamin E IU**	**Servings to get 400 IU**
NUTS		
Almonds	21 / cup	19 cups
Hazelnuts	28 / cup	14 cups
Peanuts	9 / cup	44 cups
OILS		
Olive	1.7 / Tbsp	235 Tbsp or 15.5 cups
Peanut	3.4 / Tbsp	118 Tbsp or 7.8 cups
Safflower	5.2 / Tbsp	77 Tbsp or 5.1 cups
Sesame	4 / Tbsp	100 Tbsp or 6.6 cups
Soybean	12.7 / Tbsp	31.5 Tbsp or 2.1 cups
Wheat Germ	31.6 / Tbsp	11.5 Tbsp or .77 cup
GRAINS		
Whole Wheat	3 / cup	133 cups
Millet	4 / cup	100 cups
Brown Rice	3 / cup	133 cups

Vitamin C, probably the most studied vitamin to date, requirements are suggested to be at 1,000 mg. or more. Apparently the late Dr. Linus Pauling consumed 30,000 mg. (3 grams) daily and he lived well into his ninety's and received two Nobel Prizes in his lifetime. However, to consume just 1000 mg. per day from your food supply would require the equivalent of approximately 15 oranges, everyday. I emphasize every day, because we do not store vitamin C nor do we make it.

Dr. Linus Pauling consumed 30,000 mg. daily !!

My final example is that of calcium. Newly published recommendations put daily calcium requirements at 1,000 mg and many require more. The most abundant calcium food sources are dairy products which in itself can create problems for those with dairy sensitive allergies. However, if you wanted to consume your daily calcium from food sources you would need to eat or drink:

	5 ounces of cheddar cheese	(570 Calories worth)
or	2 cups of Ricotta cheese	(860 Calories worth)
or	3 ½cups of 2% milk	(528 Calories worth)

These are minimal requirements, assuming you have no problem digesting the dairy products.

Hopefully these examples have been helpful in developing your understanding of the necessity to supplement your diet. It becomes apparent that any **complete** diet will be based on food selection, food preparation, lifestyle, immune function and responsible supplementation.

Guidelines to Supplementation

For several years now I have promoted the concept of "It's What You Don't Eat that Really Counts". The title means to imply that if we eat all the right foods or nutrients in the right quantities we will maintain better health. Here is the abridged edition of that concept.

We have difficulty in obtaining enough nutrients in the following six categories:

1. Fibre - the media has done a marvelous job of informing you of the need for more fibre in the diet and yet most North Americans still only eat twelve to thirteen (12 - 13) grams per day. Suggested protective levels are above thirty (30) grams per day of mixed fibre (Not all fibres are created equal). Adequate dietary fibre has implications for controlling blood sugar (very significant for the Better Balanced Diet), cleansing the colon and thus contributing to the prevention of colon cancer, and controlling cholesterol. Low fibre diets are associated with heart disease, cancer, diverticulosis, varicose veins, phlebitis, and obesity. Therefore, it seems wise to eat a reasonably high fibre diet and to use a quality mixed fibre supplement to ensure fibre intake is at thirty (30) grams or higher. Many try to consume more grain products (breads, cereals, pasta and the famous bran muffin) to increase their fibre intake. They often do not realize that the fibre density

> **not all fibres are created equal !!**

(grams of fibre / Calorie) is higher among many vegetables than it is among the cereal grain products. An example is the bran muffin with 0.72 grams of fibre in 40 grams and 104 Calories while one cup of broccoli contains 0.9 grams of fibre in 88 grams and 24 Calories. One slice of whole wheat bread contains 0.4 grams of fibre at 23 grams and 56 Calories while one cup of cauliflower has 0.82 grams of fibre (twice as much) in 100 grams and 24 Calories (half as many). The "Better Balanced Diet" calls for a reduction in the higher GI cereal grain foods, which many eat thinking they are healthier and higher in fibre. The GI for bran muffins is approximately 88 and whole wheat, high fibre bread is 97 while broccoli and cauliflower are in the 45 - 55 range. Even the apple, the pear or a cup of grapes with GI scores of 54, 53 and 66 respectively and 1.06, 2.32 and 0.7 grams of fibre respectively in 81, 98 and 58 Calories respectively. So the

> **The GI for high fibre bread is 97 !!**

moral is to get your fibre and low GI carbohydrates from fruits and vegetable and less from grains.

2. Minerals - again the media and advertising agencies have extolled the virtues of supplemental iron, calcium, magnesium, selenium, zinc and numerous trace minerals for many years now. Books have been written on each of these subjects. Suffice to say here, please ensure your minerals are in good supply to protect the immune system, the cardiovascular system and all your muscles and nerves. Every nerve impulse employs mineral transfers across membranes and every muscle contraction / relaxation uses calcium.

3. Antioxidants - ever since Dr. Albert Szent-Gyorgyi, the Nobel Prize winning Hungarian chemist, first synthesized vitamin C in the 1930's, the subject of "antioxidants" has been researched. Although we knew about the role citrus fruit, particularly limes, in the prevention and treatment of scurvy, it was not until vitamin C was isolated as part of the flavonoid biochemical family (there are over 500 different flavonoids in nature, sometimes referred to as bioflavonoids) that the scientists began to study the broad implications of these factors. The 1930's also marked the early vitamin E research by Doctors William and Evan Shute. Vitamin E was once described as "the vitamin looking for a purpose". Well, the scientific literature appears to have found many purposes for this elusive and sensitive antioxidant. Then of course the first recognized vitamin was named vitamin A in 1913 but it is scientifically known as retinol because it was first located in the retina of all animals. It is also found in the liver which stores about ninety per cent (90%) of the body's vitamin A . In the 1920's, vitamin A was broadly

> **In the 1920's , vitamin A was broadly linked to the immune system !!**

linked to the immune system because it was an effective infection fighter and improved the health of all tissues. It was later learned that certain plants provide large quantities of beta-carotene (one of 500 known carotenes today) known also as provitamin A from which the body makes vitamin A. Beta carotene has become more popular recently because it is a non-toxic source of vitamin A with some of its own unique antioxidant properties.

These antioxidants along with several others have become the hot bed of immune system therapy research and, as was discussed earlier in this chapter, your food supply just doesn't provide enough.

4. Essential Fatty Acids - as discussed elsewhere in this book, you need certain fats to metabolize other fats. The essential fatty acids (EFA's) are

a) alpha linolenic acid, an omega 3 fatty acid found primarily in cold pressed flax seed, walnut, soybean, pumpkin seed and canola seed oils. The **"activated"** omega 3 essential fatty acid is eicosapentaenoic acid (EPA), found primarily in cold water, blue scale fish like salmon, mackerel, herring, dogfish, trout, anchovy and sardines.

b) linoleic acid, an omega 6 fatty acid, also found in the oils listed above and in sunflower, safflower, corn oil and to a lesser extent in sesame, rice bran, peanut and almond oils. The **"activated"** omega 6 essential fatty acid is gamma linolenic acid (GLA) found in borage, evening primrose and black currant seed oils. Borage seed oil is the richest in GLA of these three oils.

Lecithin derived from the soy bean is an excellent source of both omega 3 and 6 fatty acids in addition to **choline** and **inositol** which have many complementary functions. Lecithin has recently been confirmed to provide most of the dietary choline which plays a role in memory and in physical

> **Lecithin reduces risk of cardiovascular disease by reducing cholesterol !!**

performance. According to a recent paper by Dr. David Canty, an adjunct professor in the department of nutrition and food studies at New York University, lecithin reduces risk of cardiovascular disease by lowering cholesterol through inhibiting absorption of cholesterol, increasing the excretion of cholesterol and bile acids and favorably affecting lipoprotein profiles. Lecithin is now regarded to be so important we can expect it to appear on the RDA list very soon.

The EFA's are responsible for fatty acid metabolism and for the creation of the "super hormones", prostaglandins, thromboxienes, leukotrienes, lipoxins and hydroxylated fatty acids. These "super hormones" are collectively known as the **"eicosanoids"** and every cell makes them upon demand (does not store any) if the right nutrients are available. Eicosanoids are responsible for controlling the body's hormonal system, reducing or controlling inflammation and fine tuning virtually every system in the body. **They are important!**

5. Protein - this subject is one of the most controversial in nutrition education circles. I contend that it is seriously underrated and that protein deficiencies lie at the root of many of North America's health problems. The chapter entitled "Protein is the Answer" provides the argument for increasing current protein intake recommendations by three fold. If you want to control your appetite, control your insulin levels and have healthy immune system, be sure you are eating enough high quality, easily digestible protein. (approximately one gram + / - per pound of lean body mass). The Japanese, who have the longest life expectancy in the world consume approximately three times more protein than is recommended for North Americans.

   6. Friendly Bacteria - in an age of antibiotics and other unfriendly toxic pollutants, we have difficulty in maintaining a positive "friendly bacterial" balance in the intestinal   system.   Lactobacillus   **acidophilus**   and bifidobacterium longum (**bifidus**) are the two most significant friendly   bacteria required.   The former   resides primarily   in   the alkaline   small

> # We have difficulty in maintaining a positive "friendly bacterial " balance !!

intestine and the latter is predominate in the acidic large intestine (the colon). Unfortunately, antibiotics in food and drugs do not discriminate between friendly and unfriendly bacteria. They just kill them all. Consequently many people have difficulty maintaining adequate levels of friendly bacteria necessary to complete digestion, form proper stool and activate formation of many biochemical processes in the intestinal walls. There is even evidence that adequate levels of "bifidus" in the colon reduces the risk of colon cancer.

   I suppose I should add a seventh category of nutrients deficiency   to   make   my   rationale   for   supplementation complete. **The seventh category is the B vitamins**. There are eight scientifically recognized (there are others which have yet to be recognized) B vitamins which form a **B complex**. All the B vitamins are involved in the process of extracting or releasing the energy from our food sources. In one word B complex is for **"energy"**. Unfortunately, because B vitamins are volatile and water soluble we do not store them for long. Consequently we need a constant supply throughout the day. On difficult, stress filled days, the frequency of consumption and quantity requirements increase. I always suggest that on stressful days, "graze" on B complex. A well balanced B complex supplement is one where the quantities of each vitamin appear in approximately the same **proportions** as the RDA / RNI. Any **B complex** containing 50 mg

on stressful days "graze" on B complex !!

or mcg of each nutrient is not balanced. It would contain approximately 5,000% of the RDA /RNI of vitamin B_1 and only 16% of the recommended levels for biotin. Choose a B complex where the amount of each vitamin is approximately the same per cent of the RDA /RNI for that vitamin.

Creating Your Own Supplement Program

Designing a supplement program for each reader is an impossible task. Only you, with the help of a knowledgeable health professional or counselor can decide on how much of each of the recommended nutrients will be required for you to enjoy optimum health. Keep in mind that **everybody** needs to supplement their diet for optimum metabolism, immunity and health. (**NO EXCEPTIONS!!**) When you ask for professional help, make sure the professional "walks their talk". If they don't supplement, they don't understand and will not provide you with sound advice.

Your supplement program should contain the following:

Protein Supplement
(Soy based for the isoflavones)
Multiple Vitamin / Mineral
Calcium and Magnesium
Zinc
Vitamin C
Vitamin E + selenium
(Mixed tocopherols & tocientrols)
Beta Carotene
Essential Fatty Acids
Lecithin (from Soy bean)
GLA (from Borage Seed Oil)
Bifidobacterium
Fibre   (from mixed sources to include both soluble
and insoluble fibres)
B complex (balanced according to RDA /RNI)

The list may seem formidable to you if you have never taken supplements but trust me, they are necessary for optimal health. Do not get lulled into complacency about your food

> **The body deserves complete nutrition !!**

supply. Your body deserves **complete nutrition** not generic-no-name depleted Calories. If you wish to live life to the fullest take your supplements. My advice is to become aggressive , radical and pro-active about your health. You will be glad you did.

After you have made the paradigm shift in favor of supplementation, the next question will be - which brand do

I use? I understand the confusion created by the explosion of product brands on the market. Just remember that whenever "man" processes and / or manufactures a product there will be a range in quality. There are synthetic vitamin products created from chemical cocktails that were never

Select a supplement company that conducts clinical research which gets published in peer review journals !!

alive nor did they come from food. There are relatively few actual food supplement manufacturers in North America. Many of these are "contract manufacturers" providing "turn-key" product designs for marketing companies to distribute. If you have the financial support or deep pockets, you could begin marketing your own line of product in less than six months and not even have one nutritional scientist on your staff. Now isn't that a scary prospect?

My criteria for selecting a food supplement brand are fairly simple.

1. Buy supplements from somebody who uses the supplement. In other words, they trust the brand themselves.

2. Select a supplement company which conducts clinical research (that means human studies) and has that clinical research published in "peer review" scientific journals. University scientists submit their research to these same peer review publications.

3. Use supplements that can be considered food concentrates. These are food based supplements from natural sources and processed at low temperature. There should be a satisfaction guarantee and some research to assure you that they are absorbed and really do reach the bloodstream

4. Write the company and ask for copies or a reference list of their "peer-review" published clinical research. If you don't receive anything other than sales promotional literature

you can bet they have not conducted quality clinical research. (Occasionally you may receive what appears to be clinical research but not on their product.) Be critical in your review, it is you only body .

A Final Word

If your health practitioner suggests, that supplements are not necessary because they likely will not provide you with any benefit, he or she may right. If you are

Choose the best diet possible !!

using or planning to use a generic brand, synthetic, cheap concoction, it won't do you any good. **Cheaper products that don't work are not cheaper.** Also, if you are discouraged from taking supplements by your health practitioner, ask one very significant question. "Will you be responsible for any symptoms of ill health which occur because I did not receive adequate nutrition?" I believe that advice given which discourages the use of a responsible food supplement program is a form of mal practice and requires a challenge.

Choose the best diet possible using the guidelines provided by this **Better Balanced Diet** and select and design a responsible supplement program. I know you will be happy with the results.

10

GET PHYSICAL

Man or species Homo sapiens was designed to move. Exercise is fundamental to good health. Physical exercise involving a variety of your "large" muscles has many therapeutic benefits and is absolutely necessary to ensure responsible weight management, cardiovascular health and insulin control.

The Role of Exercise

The two quickest ways to slow your metabolism and consequently gain weight or fail to lose weight are:

      1. Don't eat

and   2. Don't exercise.

The "Don't Eat" method of weight control has been tried in various ways for centuries and it still doesn't work very well.

> **If you starve yourself long enough, you will lose weight !!**

Oh yes, if you starve yourself long enough you will lose weight but you will fail your body and yourself in several ways.

First, although you metabolize Calories during starvation, many of those Calories will come from protein. Unfortunately the cortisol mechanism, described earlier in "Protein is the Answer" chapter, comes into play during starvation. Remember, this is the "carbohydrate - for - the - brain -sparing system". Cortisol does not discriminate in its protein break down activity. Consequently, in the absence of circulating amino acids, the cortisol will remove nitrogen from protein molecules in muscles, heart, liver, kidneys, lungs, blood cells and any other convenient high quality sources.

Not only does the metabolism slow down in an attempt to conserve energy and keep the blood sugar elevated enough for the brain to function but the cortisol released will lead to destruction of body functions and structures.

The other down-side of the "Don't Eat" equation is a lack of nutrients. Many nutrients are needed in good quantity and balance on a daily intake bases. Not eating means not supplying nutrients which are necessary for life. So starvation is more than inadequate Calories (energy), it also depletes all the other vital nutrients which balance hormones, produce enzymes and generally contribute to the cycles in the biology of life.

> **Those who do not exercise will metabolize less fat !!**

The "Don't Exercise" attitude of many in modern times is also a form of self destruction. First, those who do not exercise will metabolize less fat and have poor cardio-vascular-respiratory reserves leading to increases in the risk of heart attack and stroke. Second, the good cholesterol (HDL) levels tend to be lower and the insulin levels tend to be higher in the sedentary. Both of these factors are precursors to ill health.

Exercise Builds or Maintains Muscle

Muscle is active tissue which means it metabolizes food for energy. Fat cells are passive storage vessels involved in very little actual expenditure of energy. If you read the very technical chapter on fat metabolism you might remember how easily (meaning how little energy is spent) fat molecules move in and out of the fat storage cells. Consequently an exercise program involving some **progressive resistance** activity designed to build muscle is desirable in any fat management program. I emphasize "fat management" as opposed to "weight management". Body weight is a deceptive measurement. You have all heard your friend(s) or even yourself brag about having maintained the same weight as in your college years. The statement has no meaning relative to your health. Composition of that weight has much more meaning. Fat weighs less per unit of volume **muscular people metabolize** than does protein (the **more food for energy !!** major component of muscle). So naturally, a more significant measurement or measurements would be per cent body fat and / or lean body weight (fat-free body weight). Muscular people metabolize more food for energy so build strength and lose fat (not necessarily weight).

Progressive resistance exercises also metabolize fat so you not only build fat metabolizing tissue but you also metabolize fat while building that tissue. There is also evidence that progressive resistance exercise contributes to control of blood pressure, cholesterol and development or maintenance of bone density. It is never too late to begin an exercise program. Recent studies by Dr. William Evans formerly at Tufts University Center for Ageing and now Director of Nol's Physiology of Exercise Laboratory at Pennsylvania State University, demonstrated significant strength gains in seniors, aged sixty-five to ninety (65 - 90) years of age, in very short periods of time.

How much progressive resistance weight training do I need, you are likely saying to yourself? Dr. Michael Colgan suggests that the optimum muscle development occurs when you train a muscle group very intensely morning and evening of the same day, once per week. He suggests dividing (figuratively speaking of course) the body into four compartments - a)shoulders, chest, upper back, b) arms and shoulders, c) chest, back and abdominals) and d) lower back and legs. I will let you decide on what constitutes "intense" or consult a "personal trainer".

Aerobic Exercise Also Metabolizes Fat

"Aerobic" is a term meaning with oxygen or in the presence of oxygen. Most of our living - breathing hours are spent in an aerobic state where we consume adequate oxygen to generate enough energy to carry out our day to day work, recreation and sleeping tasks. The opposite to aerobic is "anaerobic"

Anaerobic metabolism occurs during extreme exertion !!

which means - in the absence of or without oxygen. Anaerobic metabolism occurs during extreme exertion when the demand for energy expenditure exceeds what we can supply through aerobic metabolism. In other words we are unable to deliver oxygen at the rate demanded by the working muscles. Fortunately we have the reserve mechanisms of anaerobic metabolism which leads to the production of lactic acid during intense exercise. During recovery, in the presence of adequate oxygen, the lactic acid is metabolized back through normal aerobic channels. A simplified schematic of these processes follows:

Aerobic Metabolism

Glycerol

Fat $\rightarrow\rightarrow\rightarrow$ Fatty Acids $\rightarrow\rightarrow\rightarrow$ Acetyl Co A + O_2 = CO_2 +

H_2O + energy

Protein $\rightarrow\rightarrow\rightarrow$ Amino Acids $\rightarrow\rightarrow\rightarrow$ Pyruvate

Carbohydrates $\rightarrow\rightarrow\rightarrow$ Glucose $\rightarrow\rightarrow$

Anaerobic Metabolism

Glycerol

Fat $\rightarrow\rightarrow\rightarrow$ Fatty Acids $\rightarrow\rightarrow\rightarrow$]

                                        ] not involved

Protein $\rightarrow\rightarrow\rightarrow$ Amino acids $\rightarrow\rightarrow\rightarrow$]

Carbohydrate $\rightarrow\rightarrow$ Glucose $\rightarrow\rightarrow\rightarrow$ Pyruvate $\rightarrow\rightarrow$ Lactic Acid

Energy

Recovery from Anaerobic Exercise

Acetyl Co A $\rightarrow\rightarrow\rightarrow$ CO_2 + H_2O + energy

Pyruvate $\leftarrow\leftarrow\leftarrow$ O_2 + Lactic Acid

I show you the above scheme simply to demonstrate that during aerobic (with oxygen) activity all three sources of energy are used as substrates. During anaerobic (without oxygen) or very intense activity only carbohydrates are used and lactic acid is produced. During recovery, the lactic acid is metabolized, in the presence of oxygen, to once again provide some of the energy and of course fats and proteins are once again utilized. Now the move from aerobic to anaerobic metabolism is not an all or none situation. There is a progressive proportional change based on intensity. As intensity increases, the proportion of aerobic energy supplied reaches a peak (known as

> **MVO_2 is a well known measure of cardiorespiratory fitness !!**

maximal oxygen consumption or MVO_2). MVO_2 is a well known measure of cardio-respiratory fitness. As intensity increases, more and more energy is supplied by the anaerobic system until this system also reaches some form of limit, then one is required to slow down and return to an all aerobic activity level.

Lactic acid accumulation not only signifies that one is approaching their exercise limits but it also inhibits the fat mobilization mechanisms. So, the "Physically Fit" person - one with a high MVO_2 - will tend to produce less lactic acid than the "less Fit". This means the "Fit" are able to metabolize more fat for longer periods of time. It really does seem to be unfair doesn't it? The "Fit" lose fat faster and for longer periods than the "Unfit".

A measurement known as the "Respiratory Exchange Ratio" (RER) is used to estimate how much carbohydrate and how much fat is being metabolized at any one time. The RER is the ratio of Carbon Dioxide (CO_2) produced per unit of oxygen (O_2) used.

$$RER = CO_2 \text{ ml} \div O_2 \text{ ml}$$

If one hundred per cent (100%) of our energy came form carbohydrate, the RER = 1 (CO_2 ml produced = O_2 ml used). If one hundred per cent (100%) of our energy came from fat the RER = 0.7 (less CO_2 ml produced than O_2 ml consumed). Naturally the RER falls between these two values during "normal" and sub-maximal activity when consuming a "mixed"diet.

Approximate Relationship of Exercise Intensity, and Fat to Carbohydrate Metabolism

RER	% MVO_2	% Calories from Fat	% Calories from Carb
1.00	100	0	100
0.95	90	15	85
0.90	80	25	75
0.85	60	50	50
0.80	40	65	35
0.75	20	85	15
0.70	5 - 10	100	0

The above chart gives no consideration to protein metabolism but we do know that as exercise is prolonged, protein can contribute up to twelve per cent (12%) of Calories at exercise intensities of sixty to sixty-five per cent (60 - 65%)

of capacity.

This brief energy metabolism discussion is merely to reinforce the need for middle range aerobic activity to encourage your body to metabolize fat. It should also reinforce one of the advantages of getting "Fit". "Fit" people use more fat during sub-maximal exercise than their less "Fit" compatriots.

The aerobic exercise at fifty to sixty-five per cent (50 - 65%) of your capacity will:

a) produce little lactic acid, thus not inhibit fat mobilization.
b) metabolize more fat than carbohydrate.
c) control circulating blood insulin levels.
d) contribute to increases in blood HDL (good cholesterol).
e) improve heart muscle strength.

and   f) lower blood pressure.

An exercise training concept, popularized by Dr. Philip Maffetone, known as "train slow to run faster" uses these aerobic principles. Although the concept is in its infancy with respect to acceptance, it is **Train slow to run faster !!** subscribed to by Mark Allen - six time Hawaiian Iron Man winner. I would encourage you to experiment with this approach. I do know that you will be happy with your weight loss and physical profile (the mirror test) if you will engage in three to four (3-4) hours per week of aerobic exercise.

Correct exercise intensity is very crucial to results in this program. Some exercise is good - more exercise may not necessarily be better. Try this method to determine your exercise intensity. -- You will need to borrow, rent or buy a reliable heart rate monitor to do this.

Your exercise intensity, as measured by your heart rate, should be approximately 180 - age in years. If you are forty (40) years of age :

180 - 40 = 140 beats per minute is your training exercise intensity.

You should have no difficulty in maintaining this intensity for thirty to sixty (30 - 60) minutes. Your biggest challenges will likely be psychological and not physical. If you have been training for some time, with progress, you may add five to ten (5 -10) beats per minute to this intensity.

Begin slowly, ten to fifteen (10 -15) minutes on the first day and four (4) days per week and progressively increase the duration. You will find after you have built an aerobic (fat burning) base that it will require more intensity to maintain this heart rate.

Please do not cheat on this one. A friend of mine with **Coaches Incorporated,** a personal lifestyle consulting company, has demonstrated many excellent results with formerly sedentary business executives and with experienced marathon runners. They experience excellent fat management and the marathon runners are improving their times.

They experience fat management and the marathon runners are improving their times !!

Coaches Incorporated experience mirrors that of Dr. Philip Maffetone and others who follow the aerobic exercise and 40 - 30 - 30 diet guidelines.

Exercise program design can be tricky if you wish to obtain optimal results. My advice is, if you feel you need help, to consult a professional who "buys-in" to the concepts of this chapter.

Finally, please understand that without exercise to help you metabolize fat, control insulin, improve muscle tone and development and to **without exercise ......you will not be successful !!** improve cardiovascular health, you will not be successful in gaining optimum health. Exercise is part of the success plan.

11

MORE GOOD STUFF

This is where I am expected to tell you, in a few words, everything I just told you in the previous ten chapters. It is usually called the summary or conclusion. Well, I am going to do a little of that, but I am also going to clarify or simplify the concepts, add to the concepts and encourage you to "keep it simple".

Summary

I basically told you that there was very little new material in this book.. I provided a historical review to demonstrate this very fact. The concept of lower carbohydrate and higher protein with responsible fat in the diet has been around for a long time. Evidence shows that prehistoric man consumed thirty per cent (30%) of his Calories in the form of protein and reduced carbohydrate food plans go back in the recent written record to the mid 1800's with

Keep it simple !!

the famous "Letter on Corpulence". I guess the historical review was to show you that I am not alone in my thinking. This review convinced me that the 40 - 30 - 30 balance in the food plan was approximately correct for most people. (remember, there is no ideal diet for species homo-sapiens).

I endorse to a large degree the work done by Dr. Barry Sears and published in his now famous "Zone" Diet. The food choices and how to obtain them are patterned after the "Zone" with some modification or liberalization.

"Technical Stuff" was inserted for the scientific

oriented reader interested in a brief layman's explanation of how fat is digested, absorbed, stored and metabolized for energy. Fat is both easy to store and easy to use for energy if the blood insulin levels are appropriately controlled. Insulin control is achieved by controlling the carbohydrate intake.

I wrote the "Science or Science?" chapter to urge you to become very critical of information perceived to be knowledge or fact. Scrutinize your sources very carefully and do a critical review of the design and conclusions reached by researchers before you "buy into " any new concept. Ask the question, is the writer an independent academic or a clinician attempting to fill his appointment book and who financed the research and was it published in a peer review journal?

How does the Better Balanced Diet differ from the Zone?
The answer to this question is fundamentally, very little. Blocks in the Zone are called Swaps in this book simply to maintain **11 Swaps per day is the minimum !!** consistency with other programs I work with. However there are some small but significant differences.

a) **Protein.** The Zone is a little conservative in the protein recommendations and I discuss this in detail in the "Protein is the Answer" chapter. It is interesting that Sears has revised his position a little since the first book by declaring **eleven** (11) blocks **(Swaps)** per day is the **minimum** requirement to meet the protein and Caloric needs of most people. If you appreciate that one Swap (block) of each contains seven (7) grams of protein and approximately ninety-one (91) Calories then eleven swaps (blocks) would provide seventy -seven (77) grams of protein and one thousand and one (1001) Calories. My recommendation of 0.75 grams of protein per pound of desirable body weight which, for a one hundred (100) pound individual, would be seventy-five (75) grams of protein and for a one hundred fifty (150) pound person it would equal one hundred twelve (112) grams.

b) **Fat choices**. The Zone constantly recommends "low fat" protein choices whereas I recommend that you eat as close to nature as possible. To elaborate, "fat-free" cheese is not natural. Many low fat and fat-free products have replaced the Calories with carbohydrate which defeats the diet plan concept. I merely recommend that if you feel that you're eating a disproportionate amount of saturated fat, increase the intake of your essential fatty acids (cold **increase your intake of essential fatty acids !!** pressed high quality oils, GLA, EPA, lecithin) to improve the metabolism of the saturated fats. You require certain fats to metabolize other fats. Yes it is advisable to select lean cuts of meat and poultry. Wild game or "grass fattened " domestic meat sources will be lower in saturated fat and in the inflammatory arachidonic acid.

c) **Whole eggs versus egg whites**. The Zone recommends egg white over whole eggs in the interest of reducing the alleged inflammatory Arachidonic Acid which is found in egg yolks. It is also the yolk that contains the cholesterol. The position taken in the Better Balanced Diet is that whole eggs are an excellent inexpensive and convenient source of many nutrients, particularly protein. An egg only contains 1.5 grams of saturated fat and 213 mg of cholesterol. I referred earlier to work which fundamentally exonerates the egg, or any other consumed cholesterol, from a causative role in elevated blood cholesterol. Sears takes on the position that eggs are "rich" in Arachidonic acid (AA) which is the precursor to PGE_2 an inflammation causing prostaglandin. However, not all PGE_2 and AA is bad. In fact the body

produces these items for a reason. They just require balance
which is where the EFA's come into play. Two large eggs
provide 142 mg of AA in 150 Calories and 12.5 grams of
protein. This is
an inexpensive | **discarding the yolk is discarding**
protein   source | **45% of the egg protein !!**
and with the
lecithin, ALA and LA in the egg much of the AA will already
be in balance.

The second defense for the whole egg is that
discarding the yolk is discarding 59 Calories, 2.78 grams of
protein (45% of the egg protein) and 1.95 grams of
monounsaturated fat. This, I consider to be a waste of
resources.

d) **Egg substitutes and liquid eggs**. The Zone makes
liberal recommendations regarding egg substitutes and liquid
egg white products. Considering the relative value of the
whole egg and the fact that substitute products are not natural,
they are not recommended in the Better Balanced Diet. The
Egg Beater product provides an alleged equivalent of nine (9)
eggs for $3.50 or more when you can buy a dozen jumbo eggs
for less than $2.00. Egg Beaters contain corn oil, not the best
oil and one associated with increasing arachidonic acid
production, aluminum sulfate, with possible implications in
Alzheimer's Disease and artificial color. These three
ingredients keep me away from Egg Beaters. When you
compare this product with eggs on a 50 ml volume equivalent,
the egg has 1.3 grams more protein and 50 more Calories, 1.8
more grams of monounsaturates and only 1.6 grams more
saturated fats. The whole egg is still good value for the dollar
and contains many valuable nutrients.

e) **Lean Body Mass**(LBM). The Zone recommends
the calculation of Fat Free Weight or Lean Body Mass before
deciding on how many grams of protein you need. I would

prefer if you merely chose your desirable body weight and used that as the criteria. After all, if you wish to be 130 pounds, you should eat like someone who weighs 130 pounds. The use of anthropometric measurements to assess body fat and therefore calculate lean body mass is predictive at the best. Margins for error in these predictions are wide and you might as well go with desirable weight. I concede the exception here is if you are considered to be obese, then by all **be aggressive with** means have a professional assess **supplementation !!** your LBM before making your protein requirement calculations.

f) **Supplementation**. Although supplementation is discussed in the Zone, it is somewhat conservative and medicinal in my mind. I am much more aggressive with responsible supplementation for two major reasons. First, as I said earlier, I have seen the results of a good supplementation program. Second, I reviewed in some detail in chapter 9 the difficulties inherent in attempting to obtain all your nutrients at protective levels from the current food supply and the Better Balance Diet is not a high Calorie diet.

g) **Food Choices in General**. I am an advocate of choosing the best diet possible and supporting it with responsible supplementation. For absolutely best results, eat organic, drink organic, avoid herbicides and pesticides, drink pure water, never eat deep fried grease in any form and do not eat at fast food outlets. I know this is radical and nobody follows these rules all of the time, but if you are aware of them and follow most of them most of the time you will be healthier.

Topics frequently discussed when starting this plan.

(a) **Distribution of fat consumption**. Prevailing wisdom suggests that a diet should receive no more than 30% of its Calories from fat and that no more than 10% of Calories should be from saturated fat. These recommendations are not inconsistent with the Better Balanced Diet which is not a ketogenic high fat diet (just

> **not all polyunsaturated acids are safe !!**

thought I would remind you). If you consume 2,000 Calories per day and 30% of those Calories are fat, that means 600 fat Calories (66 grams). Saturated fat should make up no more than 10% of Calories which equals 200 of the fat Calories (22 grams). Monounsaturated fats should make up another 10% of Calories and that leaves the last 10% of Calories for the essential fatty acids (EFA's). **In summary then, 200 Calories from fat for each of the three fat categories means approximately 22 grams of each per day.** Some authorities refer to the EFA's as polyunsaturated fats. Although the EFA's are polyunsaturated, not all polyunsaturated fatty acids are essential. There is a difference. Many polyunsaturated fatty acids are rancid because they are very unstable and many have become the toxic trans fatty acids. Choose your fats and oils carefully.

(b) **Calories are not counted first !** The error many will make in assessing this diet will be to take an example of Calorie expectations and decide that the protein level is too high or will calculate the Calorie intake based on the number of recommended Swaps and declare the Calorie count too low. An example tried on me a year ago was "if the protein should be 30% of Calories, then somebody on a 5,000 Calorie diet will require :

5,000 x 0.3 = 1500 protein Calories ÷ 4 = 375 grams of protein. The fallacy to this argument is that very few athletes need 5,000 Calories per day and second is the need to understand that if the Calories consumed are of high density nutrients as recommended in this program, then fewer Calories are necessary.   Caloric requirements were established by

> **with high density nutrition, fewer Calories are needed !!**

assessing how many Calories were consumed by a variety of people in a variety of tasks and deciding that was what was needed. No consideration was given to the quality of those Calories nor the range of mechanical efficiency demonstrated in a wide variety of people.

(c) **Too much protein critique**. Without beating a topic into oblivion, I remind you of the material presented in the chapter "Protein is the Answer". The protein levels recommended in this program present no threat to kidney function, calcium absorption, nor to liver function. In fact, these levels will likely help liver and kidney repair because the amino acids of protein along with vitamin C, beta carotene and the essential fatty acids are necessary for any organ to rebuild and repair tissue.

(d) **Protein and essential fatty acids.** Essential fatty acids were discussed in their role for producing and maintaining the quantity and balance of the eicosanoids but little was said about their relationship to high quality protein. Work conducted by German scientists and carried on by Dr. Johanna Budwig (referred to in "Fats that Heal and Fats that Kill" by Udo Erasmus) demonstrated the health giving values of increasing the consumption of high quality protein in the presence of high quality essential fatty acids. She used yogurt and kwark in combination with cold pressed flax seed (linseed) oil in her experiments. The significance of this century old work is just now becoming evident. You require both protein and EFA"s to build

high quality protein with high quality EFA's !!

hormones, particularly the super hormones known as the eicosanoids.

(e) **Protein stimulates insulin also**. The issue of higher protein intake possibly contributing to the problem of elevated insulin because protein does stimulate the pancreas to release insulin was partially addressed, indirectly, in the "Historical Stuff" chapter. In that chapter a graph on page 35 demonstrates the relatively low level of insulin stimulation provided by protein. Glucagon, the other pancreatic hormone which is partially responsible for mobilizing fat, is also released in response to protein intake so a balance occurs.

(f) **40 -30 -30 Exceptions**. There are two places where, **at the moment,** I still endorse a variation away from the 40 -30- 30 plan. The first occurs before and during an event of high intensity which lasts for over one hour of continuous exercise (a marathon race, an Iron Man Triathlon, other triathons, 100 mile or century runs, etc.). Under these conditions many have found it useful to pre-load with a high carbohydrate drink in the one to two hours prior to the event and to continue to use high quality sport drink during the event. The second exception immediately follows an intense physical activity when the muscles are "screaming" to be refueled with both carbohydrates and branched chain amino acids. Failure to re-load the muscles quickly usually results in stiff and achy muscles. To avoid these unpleasantries research has shown that consumption of a high quality source of branched chain amino acids (in the form of a whey protein isolate) in the presence of a glucose polymer (not just simple sugar) in a ratio of 2.7 to 1 in favor of the polymer has been very effective. This mixture should be consumed immediately after the cessation of exercise (Based on research published in the Journal of Applied Physiology in January of 1992 by Dr. John Ivy's laboratory at The University of Texas.)

(g) **Exercise and insulin resistance**. Physical activity, even if it is non-vigorous physical activity such as walking, can lower the risk for developing diabetes, according to an item in the March 4th ,1998 issue of "The Journal of the American Medical Association (JAMA). Previous studies had linked vigorous physical activity to reduced incidence of Type II diabetes, but the benefits of moderate **failure to reload the muscles, results in stiffness aches & pains !!** intensity physical activity had been unclear. These findings are consistent with the directions of the Better Balanced Diet. The objective is to maintain control over the blood insulin levels through wise food choices and through aerobic, fat-burning exercise.

(h) **Keep it Simple and do not become Paranoid.** No diet can be considered universally ideal for species homo sapiens. However, it appears that in excess of 75% of North Americans can benefit from a 40 - 30 -30 program designed to control their blood insulin levels. The beauty of a program designed to control your hormonal mechanisms is that it occurs almost immediately. That is why I suggest you try one week of balanced protein drinks combined with meal replacement bars as soon as possible. This, easy to obtain balance will demonstrate to you the effectiveness of the 40 - 30 - 30 balance. The backbone of this plan is enough protein and protein in every meal and every snack combined with low glycemic index carbohydrates. Low GI carbohydrates tend to be fresh vegetables and fruit which also have a high density of nutrition compared the high GI, low density nutrient grains. That is the simplicity of this plan. Do not make it any more complicated.

If you are hungry, follow the rules of the plan, have another snack and do not confound the pancreas by mixing in or sneaking a high GI snack for a quick fix. **If you are going to digress, use fat or fat+protein items because they are insulin neutral.** Dr. Bob Arnot uses an expression I like and that is "forward plan" your eating. In other word make sure the refrigerator contains convenient "good" snack combinations.

(i) **If you digress from the plan**, the consequences will be felt immediately, but you can return to balance in a very few hours simply by following the guidelines of this plan.

(j) **Carbohydrate requirements.** Skeptics who have been indoctrinated in the "carbohydrates for energy" school will be concerned as to the carbohydrate supply in this plan. First, there is no RDA/RNI for carbohydrates. Second, the only time you deplete your muscles of carbohydrates is if you exercise at high intensity for an hour or more. **You are always using fat !!** Routinely, you are always using fat to supply some of your energy, except during high intensity exertion. The fat metabolizing mechanism is an ideal carbohydrate saving system. The Inuit (Eskimo) lived for centuries in the frozen north with access to very few carbohydrates. In fact, the greatest health problems in that northern population developed after they were introduced to the high carbohydrate food choices of their southern "civilized" neighbors.

A friend who has been a support worker for Diabetics shared the following advice regarding ideal carbohydrate intake for a Diabetic. This guideline was used over 40 years ago by one of the attending Physicians she worked with. The recommended carbohydrate intake was 10% of Calories in grams. For example, if you consumed 1,000 Calories the carbohydrate portion would or should be
1,000 Calories x .10 = 100 grams x 4 = 400 Calories
which would be 40% of Calories. (Isn't that interesting -- over 40 years ago he was offering this advice for insulin control)

(k) **Losing Fat**. Fat can only leave the body in one of two ways: first , is by way of energy metabolism where nine (9) Calories of energy are provided with every gram of fat; and second, under the condition of ketosis some ketone bodies, which represent partially metabolized fat molecules, are excreted without providing energy

> **Fat can only leave the body in one of two ways!!**

for physical work. In the absence of ketosis, it require 3500 Calories of energy expenditure to account for one pound of fat. That means you still need a Caloric deficit of 3500 Calories to lose one pound of fat. In the absence of starvation (which was previously discussed as a bad idea) you can likely, in reality, **only effectively lose 1.5 to 2 pounds of fat per week.** I would only recommend the ketosis method for short periods in the obese.

(l) **Water loss**. Many critics of higher protein diets will attribute the weight loss to water loss. This explanation only holds so much water, before it loses credibility. First, there is approximately three (3) grams of water obligated by every gram of carbohydrate (glycogen) stored. Glycogen stores can, in carbohydrate loaded athletes, reach Seven

This explanation only holds so much water!!

hundred to nine hundred (700 - 900) grams which would obligate 2100 to 2700 grams of water. This water would represent 5 to 6 pounds of water at the most. To lose six pounds of water due to carbohydrate depletion would require exhaustive exercise to deplete most of the muscles of all glycogen or starvation.

A second water loss explanation can be that with a lower insulin level, brought on by lower carbohydrate intake, the kidneys are not instructed to retain sodium which also obligates a certain amount of water per gram. This water loss would not be a negative health response but rather a positive response by lowering blood pressure.

(m) **Cravings and hunger**. A frequently asked question is "how to I get over craving certain foods, particularly the carbohydrates (sweets and breads)?" The most common solution deals with the balance and completeness of your diet. If you are following the 40 - 30 - 30 plan carefully and still experiencing cravings, you likely need to look at your nutrient choices. Most of your carbohydrates should come from vegetables and fruit (high nutrient density foods) to ensure a good supply of vitamins and minerals. Second, you may need to adjust your **supplement** intake to complete the nutrient requirements for your body.

A couple of examples will serve to punctuate this

point. It has been known for years that if you **crave chocolate** you are likely deficient in calcium and / or magnesium - a very common nutritional deficiency in the modern world. If you **crave sweets**, you are likely deficient in protein - another common deficiency. If you cannot eat enough high protein foods, or preparation of high protein foods take too long for your busy lifestyle, use a high quality **protein supplement** derived from a soy protein isolate so you take advantage of the isoflavones which offer many health benefits.

> **If you crave sweets you are likely protein deficient!!**

(n) **Constipation and irregularity**. This is a common problem for those unaccustomed to eating higher protein diets. The explanation can usually be found in the level of fibre intake. Many people seem to reduce their fibre when beginning this program because they have reduced the intake of breads, muffins and pasta but have not yet replaced them with "good" carbohydrate sources. I suggest a good quality - multiple source - fibre supplement and the use of a gentle herbal laxative which will really be a blood purifier which has the coincidental effect of a laxative. **DO NOT USE COMMERCIAL LAXATIVES WITHOUT YOUR DOCTOR'S PRESCRIPTION.**

(o) **Difficulty losing weight.** If you have correctly calculated your protein requirements, converted it to swaps and have followed it diligently but still so not lose weight, you may need to fine tune your valance choices. Try reducing the carbohydrate swaps by one and replace it with protein and good fat. If that still doesn't work, repeat this exercise until it does. Dr. Calvin Ezrin in his **Endocrine Control Diet** refers to this concept as means of establishing your **carbohydrate tolerance** level. After you start losing weight at a desirable rate, you can experiment by re-introducing the carbohydrate swaps by increasing by on swap per week. If you start to gain, or plateau, you have reached your carbohydrate tolerance level - cut back again. Finding your carbohydrate tolerance level may be an ongoing exercise. As you become healthier through eating the Better Balanced Diet way, exercising and supplementing, your carbohydrate tolerance level may change.

(p) **Plateaus**. One of the many frustrations frequently experienced during weight loss programs is that of losing weight for a period of time followed by a stall in weight loss. Several explanations for this phenomenon have appeared in the literature over the years.

One possibility is you need to review your food swap requirements and be sure that your protein and carbohydrate levels are correct.

A second possibility is that you may have accumulated a few toxins over the years. These toxins (please don't ask me to identify them by name) MAY interfere with certain metabolic processes which in turn inhibit the metabolism of fat. Part of the solution would be to drink more water (purified is best to ensure you are not introducing more toxins) and use a cleansing herbal laxative supplement.

> **Toxins may interfere with fat metabolism!!**

You might also need a good fibre supplement to cleanse the colon and prevent toxins from recycling throughout your system.

A third possibility is the need to perform a little or a little more aerobic - fat burning - exercise.

(q) **How rigid?** We all have slightly different nutrient needs based on our genetics(DNA), environment and experience with the world. If your weight is out of control or your health is terrible or your energy is non-existent, then you need to be very rigid with the recommendations of this eating plan. However, others can be more liberal or approximate and estimate combinations based on the general rules set out in the "Let's Eat " chapter. However, if you don't feel great or lose some weight (assuming you need to) by estimating , don't quit, get more specific about grams and per cent.

(r) **Planning meals and food choices**. It has been suggested that most people have a narrow selection of favorite meals. Think about it. How many different menu items are in your breakfast, lunches, dinners and snacks. Take the time to evaluate these most common choices and proceed to "tweek" the combinations so they become balanced according the guidelines in this eating plan. There are only a few foods that I believe you should eliminate and they were described earlier. Just take each of your most common meals and check the protein - carbohydrate - fat levels (convert to a per cent of Calories) and check the protein to carbohydrate ratio. If your choices are out of balance, adjust each meal by adding or subtracting portions of each of the macro-nutrients.

> **Control of blood insulin levels is the major mission statement !!**

(s) **The Ultimate Mission Statement**. Control of blood insulin levels is the major mission statement of this eating plan. The second mission statement is to enhance the balance of hormone and super hormone (eicosanoids) production. The third mission statement is to be sure you consume adequate protein.

Control of blood insulin is achieved by maintaining the ratio of protein to carbohydrate intake between 0.6 and 0.95 with 0.75 considered ideal. It is also advisable to minimize the consumption of undesirable (high glycemic index) carbohydrates.

Hormonal balance will be achieved by controlling insulin production and consuming thirty per cent (30%) or

> **Control of insulin by maintaining the ratio of protein to carbohydrate !!**

your Calories as high quality fats (10% essential fatty acids, 10% Monounsaturated fatty acids and no more than 10% saturated fatty acids).

Adequate protein intake can be achieved by eating protein in every meal and every snack (have you read this one before?), but no more than thirty-five to forty (35 - 40) grams per sitting. This habit will contribute to insulin control and provide the building blocks for hormonal production.

(t) **Before you eat that carbohydrate**. To control the glycemic index response of carbohydrate foods always try to each part of the protein portion of you meal or snack first. Always eat some cheese or meat before that first drink of wine ore beer. If appetizers are served, look for the high protein variety first. If you want a sweet treat, precede it with a slice of chicken, turkey or corned beef. **Try to control that glycemic index response and you will feel the difference.**

(u) **Enjoy Great Health**. The objective of elaborating this plan is to help you enjoy optimum health. The biological mechanisms at work are very complicated but you don't have to worry about them because the science, which has been developing for years, behind these eating choices is sound. The diet plans which are standing the test of time are the

"Higher " protein and "Lower" carbohydrate with " Good" fat food choice plans.

So shift your paradigm, choose your food carefully, exercise and supplement to enjoy **Great Health.**

Shift your paradigm, choose your food carefully !!

SOME GOOD RESOURCES

The Protein Counter by Annette B. Natow and Jo-Ann
    Heslin, Pocket Books, New York, 1997.
    Provides a comprehensive list of Calorie, Protein,
    Carbohydrate and Fat content of a wide range of
    foods including brand names.

Nutrition Almanac edit by John Kirschmann of Nutrition
    Search Inc.
    Provides a comprehensive "Table of Food
    Composition".

www.nal.usda.gov/fnic/cgi
    Access to the USDA **food composition** data base

www.nutribase.com
    A web site by Cybersoft Inc. listing nutrient
        composition of **19,344 food items** plus **3,160
menu   items from 71 restaurants .**

www.olen.com/food
    A web site by Olen Publishing which lists under "food
    finder" a comprehensive list of **fast food facts**
    according the Minnesota Attorney Generals office.

http://gate.cruzio.com/~mendosa/diabetes.htm
    Rick Mendosa maintains a personal web page but
    provide a very comprehensive **Glycemic Index** list.

www.karenskitchen.com
    provides **menu items, recipes, and support**
    information for following the 40 - 30 - 30 meal plans

BIBLIOGRAPHY

Arnot, R. **Dr. Bob Arnot's Guide to Turning Back the Clock**. Little Brown and Company. Boston, MA. 1995.

Atkins, R.C. **Dr. Atkins' New Diet Revolution.** Avon Books, New York, NY. 1997.

Banting, W. "Letter on Corpulence" self published. 1864.

Bland, J. **Medical Application of Clinical Nutrition**. Harper and Row. New York, NY. 1983.

Boode-Peterson, T.H. Energy News Updates: Project 2000 Inc. Boylston, MA. Fall 1993.

Brillat-Savarin, Jean-Anthelme. "Preventative or Curative Treatment of Obesity." an essay in **The Physiology of Taste** 1825.

Brown, E.D. et.al. "Plasma Carotenoid in normal men after a single ingestion of vegetables or purified beta carotene." **American Journal of Clinical Nutrition**. 49,1258-1265, 1989

Canty, D.C. "Lecithin and choline redeemed." **Nutrition Science News**. October 1997.

Chaitow, Leon. **Amino Acids in Therapy**. Thorsons Publishers Inc. Rochester, VT. 1985

Cheraskin, E., W. Ringsdorf and F.H. Medford. "The ideal daily intake of threonine, valine, phenylalanine, leucine, isoleucine and methionine." The **Journal of Orthomolecular Psychiatry**. 7, 150-155, 1978.

Cheraskin, E., W.M. Ringsdorf, Jr., and F.H. Medford. "The ideal daily total protein intake." **Journal of the Medical Association of the State of Alabama.** Nov. 1977.

Clement, D.B., R.C. Asmundson and C.W. Medhurst. "Hemoglobin values: comparative survey of the 1976 Canadian Olympic team." **Canadian Medical Association   Journal**. 117, 614-616, 1977.

Colgan, M. **Optimum Sports Nutrition**. Advanced Research Press. New York, NY. 1993.

D'Adamo, J. **The D'Adamo Diet.** McGraw-Hill, New York,   NY. 1989.

Eades, M.R. and M.D. Eades. **Protein Power**. Bantam Books. New York, NY. 1996.

Eaton, S.B. et.al. "An evolutionary perspective enhance understanding of human nutritional requirements." **Journal of Nutrition.** 126, 1732-1740, 1996.

Erasmus, U. **Fats that Heal and Fats that Kill**. Alive Books. Vancouver, BC. 1995

Ezrin, C. and R.E. Kowalski. **The Endocrine Control Diet**. Harper Row. New York, NY. 1990.

Fast, J. **The Omega - 3 Breakthrough**. The Body Press.

Tucson, AZ. 1987.

Firmma E. Baer Report, Rutgers University, **Firmament Farming Magazine**. 1991.

Fredericks, C. **Carlton Fredericks' Program for Living** Longer. Simon and Schuster. New York, NY. 1983.

Fredericks, C. **Dr. Carlton Fredericks' Low-Carbohydrate Diet**. Universal-Award House. New York, NY. 1965.

Gittleman, A.L and J.M. Desgrey. **Beyond Pritikin**. Bantam Books. New York, NY. 1989.

Gittleman, A.L., J. Templeton and C. Versace. **Your Body Knows Best**. Pocket Books. New York, NY. 1996.

Gold, R., and K. Rose-Gold. **The Good Fat Diet**. Bantam Books. Toronto, ON. 1987.

Gorbach, S.L. and B.R. Goldin. "Nutrition and the Gastrointestinal Microflora." **Nutrition Reviews**. 50, 378-381, 1992.

Heller, R.F., and R.F. Heller. **Healthy for Life**. Penguin Books. New York, NY. 1995.

Heller, R.F., and R.F. Heller. **The Carbohydrates Addict's Diet**. Penguin Books. New York, NY. 1993.

Himsworth, H.P. "Diabetes mellitus: its differentiation into insulin-sensitive and insulin-insensitive types." **Lancet**. 127-130, 1936.

Jenkins, D.J.A. et.al. "Glycemic index of foods: a physiological basis for carbohydrate exchange." **American Journal of Clinical Nutrition**. 34, 362-366, 1981.

Jensen, C.D. et.al. "Repletion and depletion of serum alpha and beta carotene in humans with carrots and a algae-derived supplement." **Acta Vitaminol Ensymol**. 7, 189- 198, 1985.

Keys, A., J.T. Anderson, and F. Frande. "Serum cholesterol response to changes in the diet. II. The effect of cholesterol in the diet, **Metabolism,** 14, 759, 1965.

Krehl, W. "Vitamin Supplementation: A practical View." distributed by Vitamin Information Services, Nutley, NJ. 1989

Krogh, A. and M. Krogh. Meddelser om Grönland. 51, 1914.

Lambert-Lagacé, L. and M. Laflamme. **Good Fat / Bad Fat**. Stoddart Publishing. Toronto, ON. 1995.

Lieberman, S. and N. Bruning. **The Real Vitamin & Mineral Book**, second edition. Avery Publishing Group. Garden City Park, NY. 1997.

Maffetone, Philip. **In Fitness and in Health: Everyone is an athlete**. David Barmore Productions. Stamford, NY.1994

Maffetone, Philip. **Training for Endurance**. David Barmore Productions. Stamford, NY. 1996.

Matsuzaki, T. "Longevity, diet and nutrition in Japan: epidemiological studies." **Nutrition Reviews**. 50, 355-359, 1992.

Miller, B. **Food Supplements : No Longer an Option**. Bruce Miller Enterprises Inc. Dallas, TX. 1996.

Pauling, L. **Vitamin C and the Common Cold**. Bantam Books. New York, NY.1974.

Puhn, A. **The 5 - Day Miracle Diet**. Ballantine Books. New York, NY. 1996.

Reaven, G.M. "Role of insulin resistance in human disease." **Diabetes**. 37, 1595-1607, 1989.

Reuben, C. **Antioxidants: Your Complete Guide** .Prima Publishing. Rocklin, CA. 1995.

Sears, B. **Zone Perfect Meals in** Minutes. Regan Books / Harper Collins. New York, NY. 1997.

Sears, B. **Mastering the Zone**. Regan Books / Harper Collins New York, NY. 1997.

Sears, B and B. Lawren, **Enter the Zone**. Regan Books / Harper Collins. New York, NY. 1995

Sheats, C., and M. Greenwood-Robinson. **Lean Bodies**. The Summit Group. Fort Worth, TX. 1992.

Simopoulos, A.P. and J. Robinson. **The Omega Plan**. Harper Collins. New York, NY. 1998.

Stillman, I.M. and S.S. Baker. **The Doctor's Quick Weight Loss Diet**. Dell Publishing. New York, NY. 1968.

Tarnower, H. and S.S. Baker. **The Complete Scarsdale Medical Diet**. Rawson Wade Publishers. New York, NY. 1979.

Tolstoi, E. "The effect of an exclusive mat diet on the chemical constituents of the blood," **Journal of Biological Chemistry**. 83, 753-758, 1929.

Williams, R. **Biochemical Individuality**. Wiley and Sons. New York, NY. 1956.

Worthington-Roberts, B. et.al. "Supplementation Patterns of Washington State dieticians." **Journal of the American Dietetic Association**. 84, 795--799, 1984.

Young, V. , D.M. Bier and P.L. Pellett. "A theoretical basis for increasing current estimates of the amino acid requirements in adult man, with experimental support." **American Journal of Clinical Nutrition**. 50, 80-92, 1989.

Yudkin, J. "Sugar intake and myocardial infarction." **American Journal of Clinical Nutrition**. May, 503, 1967

Yudkin, J. and M. Carey. "The treatment of obesity by the 'high-fat' diet." The inevitability of calories." **Lancet**, 2, 939-941, 1960.

Yudkin, J. "Dietary factors in arteriosclerosis: sucrose," **Lipids**. 13, 370-72, 1978

Yudkin, J. **The Slimming Business**. The Macmillan Company. New York, NY. 1959

Yudkin, J. **Sweet and Dangerous.** Bantam Books, New York, NY. 1972.

Zawadzki, K.M., B.B. Yaspelkis III and J.L. Ivy. "Carbohydrate-protein complex increases the rate of muscle glycogen storage after exercise." **Journal of Applied Physiology**. 72, 1854-1859, 1992.

INDEX

Acidophilus 134
Adipose tissue 49, 50, 52, 57, 66, 68
Adrenaline 67
Adrenal Glands 76
Aerobic exercise 142, 146, 148
Alertness 62, 73, 89
Almonds 90, 98, 103-105, 110-112, 128
American Journal of Clinical Nutrition 38, 74, 78, 161, 164,
Amino acids 71, 76, 77, 139, 155, 156, 161
Amino Acids in Therapy 77, 161
Anabolic 66, 82
Anaerobic Exercise 143
Antioxidants 126, 131, 132, 165
Appetite 66, 69, 75, 81, 134
Apples 37, 98
Arachidonic Acid 93, 96, 151, 152
Arnot, Dr. Bob 36, 158, 161
Asparagus 99, 110, 111
Athletes 9, 14, 39, 41, 75, 81, 155
Atkins, Dr. Robert 11, 28, 29, 31, 32, 37, 88, 161
ATP 47

Back bacon 1 00, 103-106, 108, 112
Bacon 98, 100, 103-106, 108, 112
Bacteria 134
Bagels 96
Bananas 88, 96
Banting , William   29, 30, 32, 161
Barley 100
Bass 100
Beans 99, 100, 108, 110, 117
Beef 28, 72, 90, 98-100, 105, 109, 111, 112, 117
Beer 28, 86, 88, 100, 112, 122
Beets 96, 100
Beta carotene 126, 127, 132, 136, 155, 161, 164
Better Balanced Diet 9, 13, 27, 40, 73, 81, 83, 85, 89, 90, 115, 130,
                138, 150-152, 154, 157,162
Bifidus 134

Blood pressure 67, 68, 70, 81, 86, 141, 146
Blood stream 5 9, 64, 65, 68, 69
Blood sugar 38, 56, 61, 63, 65, 66, 69, 76, 130, 140
Blueberries 100, 103-106
Body fat 3, 39, 44, 62, 141, 153
Body weight 86, 141, 151, 153
Bok choy 99
Borage oil 94
Brain 56, 76, 139, 140
Bread 28, 37, 88, 91, 96, 99, 100, 103, 105-109, 111, 112, 123, 130,
              131
Breakfast 38, 116, 117
Broccoli 99, 109, 110, 124, 130, 131
Brussels sprouts 99, 110, 111
Butter 11, 48, 98, 103, 104, 112, 118
B complex 135, 136

Cabbage 99, 100, 123
Calamari 100, 112
Calcium 23, 72, 80-82, 126, 129, 131, 136, 155
Calories 13, 30, 31, 39, 40, 54, 55, 58, 77, 81, 82, 89, 93, 96, 112, 114,
                115, 122, 129-131, 136, 139, 140, 145, 149-152, 154,
                155, 159, 166
Cancer 37, 41, 126, 130, 134
Candy bar 100
Cantaloupe 98, 100, 103-106, 109, 112, 126
Canty, Dr. David 133, 161

Carbohydrates 2, 17, 20, 24, 27, 29, 30, 32, 34, 36-41, 48, 50, 51, 55,
                57, 59, 68-70, 73-75, 85, 87-89, 95-97, 115, 131, 144,
                156-158, 160,162
Carbohydrate swaps 96, 161
Carrots 38, 88, 90, 96, 100, 126, 127, 164
Catfish 100
Cauliflower 99, 100, 109, 111, 130, 131
Celery 99, 100, 106, 108, 112
Cereal 11, 28, 38, 91, 100, 130
Chaitow, Dr. Leon 77, 161
Cheese 87, 88, 90, 91, 98, 99, 103-113, 117, 118, 129, 151
Cherries 100
Chicken 90, 98, 99, 105-107, 109, 110, 112
Chili 108, 110

Cholesterol 11, 12, 15, 20, 23-25, 30, 45, 48, 51, 66-69, 86, 130, 133,
               140, 141, 146, 151, 164
Chronic Fatigue 75
Clams 100
Cod 100
Colon cancer 130, 134
Corn 38, 90, 96, 100, 133, 152
Corned beef 98, 100, 112
Cortisol 76, 139, 140
Cortisone 76
Cottage cheese 98, 99, 103, 105, 112
Crackers 38, 100
Cranberries 98, 110, 111
Cravings 65
Cream 100
Cucumber 100

Dairy products 129
Dates 100
Diabetes 6, 51, 52, 61, 62, 157, 163, 165
Dieticians 121, 123, 166
Dinner 29, 100, 111, 116, 117
Disease 9-12, 14, 19, 20, 23-25, 37, 62, 63, 68, 74, 75, 78, 80, 94, 125,
               126, 130, 133, 152, 165
Dr. Atkins' New Diet Revolution 161
Dressing 106, 107, 109, 111
Duck 99

Eades, Dr. Michael & Dr. Mary Dan 14, 36-44, 73, 88, 162
Eaton, Dr. S. Boyd 79, 162
Eggplant 99
Egg Beaters 152
Egg white 151, 152
Egg yolk 11
Eicosanoids 68, 70, 91, 92, 133, 155, 156
Eicosapentaenoic acid (EPA) 92
English muffins 99
Enter the Zone 10, 41, 42, 44, 165
Enzymes 46, 53, 56, 58, 140
Erasmus, Dr. Udo 44, 92, 93, 155, 162
Eskimos 30, 43, 80
Exercise 1, 10, 13, 21, 23, 26, 28, 33-36, 38, 40, 44, 48, 53, 55-57, 59,

67, 76, 77, 82, 86, 90, 139-148, 156-159, 167
Ezrin, Dr. Calvin 31, 32, 37, 42, 88, 161

Fast food 122, 153
Fats that Heal and Fats that Kill 92, 155, 162
Fatty acids 9, 13, 39, 40, 44, 45, 47-52, 57, 58, 66-71, 80, 92-94, 97,
        132, 133, 136, 143, 151, 154, 155
Fat burning 9, 44, 90, 147
Fat cells 49, 50, 52, 140
Fat swaps 96
Fibre 44, 97, 130, 131, 136
Fish 79, 87, 90, 91, 96, 98, 100, 109-111, 113, 132
Fredericks, Dr.Carlton 29, 31, 80, 163
Fructose 89
Fruit juices 96
Fruit 90, 96, 97, 100-105, 112, 113, 124, 125, 131, 157

Gamma linolenic acid (GLA) 133
Garlic 106, 107
Genetics 14, 23, 25, 62, 77
Gittleman, Ann Louise 11, 14, 39, 42, 44, 163
Glucagon 48, 52, 59, 62, 65, 66, 70, 91, 92
Glucose 46, 47, 49, 51-53, 56-59, 61, 62, 64-66, 156
Glycemic index (GI) 38, 64
Glycogen 55-58, 62, 66, 167
Gold, Dr. Robert 163
Gorbach, Dr. Sherwood L. 74, 163
Grains 7, 9, 13, 88, 100, 113, 127, 128, 131, 157
Grapefruit 98, 100, 104, 105, 117
Grapes 98, 103, 108, 112, 131
Growth hormone 66, 67, 69
Guacamole 107, 108, 112

Haddock 100
Halibut 100
Ham 98, 100, 105-107, 112, 117
HDL Cholesterol 68
Headaches 65
Healthy for Life 14, 36, 37, 70, 163
Heart attack 140
Heart disease 10-12, 19, 20, 23-25, 68, 126, 130
Heart rate 67, 147

Heller Dr. Richard & Dr. Rachael 32, 163
Hemoglobin 75, 81, 82, 162
Herbs 97, 110, 111
High blood pressure 81, 86
Honey 100
Hormones 62, 67, 68, 91, 133, 140, 156
Human growth hormone 66
Humus 100
Hunger 65
Hyperinsulinemia 37, 62, 63
Hypoglycemia 56, 86

Ice cream 100
Immune system 68, 73, 74, 131, 132, 134
Inflammation 68, 69, 86, 133, 152
Insulin levels 33, 51, 61, 65-68, 134, 140, 146, 150, 157
Insulin 1, 14, 20, 25, 29, 32-36, 38-42, 48, 51, 52, 56, 58, 59, 61-70, 75,
        91, 92, 134, 139, 140, 146, 148, 150, 156-159, 163,
        165
Inuit 15, 80, 158
In Fitness and in Health 14, 41, 164
Iron 76, 131, 146, 156
Ivy 167

Jenkins, Dr. D.J.A. 38, 163
Jensen, Chris 127, 164

Ketones 54
Ketosis 28, 52, 54
Keys, Dr. Ancel 12, 20, 23, 24, 164
Kidneys 67, 69, 83, 140
Kidney beans 99, 108, 110
Kiwi 100, 106, 108, 112

Lamb 100
Lean Bodies 39, 48, 165
Lean body mass 95, 134, 153
Lecithin 93, 96, 133, 136, 151, 152, 161
Leeks 99
Lemon 100, 106, 107, 109-111
Letter on Corpulence 29, 149, 161
Lettuce 99, 100, 106-108

Leukotrienes 68, 133
Lieberman, Shari 127, 164
Life expectancy 79, 134
Linoleic acid 92, 93, 133
Lipoxins 133
Liver 45, 49, 51-53, 56-59, 62, 66, 68, 69, 72, 80, 81, 101, 132, 140,
    155
Lobster 100, 107
Low blood sugar 56
Lunch 116, 117

Macadamia nuts 98, 105, 107, 111
Maffetone, Dr. Philip 14, 41, 42, 146, 147, 164
Magnesium 23, 82, 123, 131, 136
Malnutrition 74, 75, 83
Mango 100
Margarine 11, 96
Mastering the Zone 42, 43, 165
Matsuzaki 78, 164
Mayonnaise 98, 106, 108, 112
Meat 30, 80, 87, 88, 91, 97, 98, 100, 104, 105, 108-112, 118, 151
Melba toast 100
Metabolic rate 82
Metabolism 13, 23, 40, 47, 50, 51, 57, 69, 77, 82, 91, 133, 135, 139,
    140, 142-146, 151, 164
Milk 72, 89-91, 99, 112, 113, 129
Miller, Dr. Bruce 119, 165
Minerals 71, 82, 122, 131
Muscles 36, 56-58, 66, 81-82, 131, 139-142, 156, 158
Mushrooms 99, 100, 106-108, 110

Nectarine 106, 111
Norepinephrine 67
Nutrition Reviews 74, 78, 163, 164
Nuts 96, 98, 102, 105, 107, 111, 114, 117, 127, 128

Oatmeal 37, 99, 100, 103, 104, 112
Obesity 6, 7, 31, 130, 161, 166
Olives 96, 102, 106, 112
Olive oil 94, 98, 103, 104, 108, 110, 117, 118
Onions 99, 106, 107, 109-111
Oranges 98, 129

Osteoporosis 72, 80
Overweight 7, 31, 95
Oxidation 52, 57, 68
Oxygen 41, 57, 82, 142, 144, 145

Pancreas 52, 53, 59, 61-66, 70, 156, 158
Pantothenic acid 77
Papaya 100
Parsnips 96, 100
Pauling, Dr. Linus 129, 165
Peaches 98, 104, 105, 107, 110
Peanuts 98, 102, 106, 112, 128
Peanut butter 98, 103, 104, 112
Pears 98
Peas 99-101
Pepperoni 100
Physical acitivity 90
Plums 98
Polyunsaturated fats 154
Pork 98, 100, 109, 111
Potassium 82
Potatoes 27, 38, 88, 90, 96, 99, 100, 104, 105, 126, 127
Potato chips 100
Poultry 113, 151
Prostacyclins 68
Prostaglandins 68, 92, 133
Protein powder 89, 103, 104, 112,161
Protein swaps 96, 115
Prunes 100
Puhn, Adele 38, 165

Raisins 38, 88, 96, 100
Raspberries 98, 100, 103-106, 112
RDA 120,158
Reaven, Dr.Gerald 62, 165
Recommended Daily Allowance (RDA) 120
Recommended Nutrient Intake (RNI) 120
Restaurant 71, 91
Reuben, Carolyn 165
Rice 38, 88, 90, 91, 96, 100, 128, 133
Rice cakes 38
Ricotta cheese 99, 129

RNI 120,158
Running 41, 75

Salami 100
Salisbury Steak 30
Salmon 55, 93, 96, 100, 106, 108, 111, 132
Salt 98
Sardines 133
Saturated fats 151, 152
Sauerkraut 99
Scallops 107
Seafood 106, 107
Sears, Dr. Barry   10, 13, 15, 41, 42, 44, 69, 85, 87, 90, 149-151, 165
Selenium 127, 131, 136
Sesame oil 104
Shaklee 33
Sheats Cliff   39, 48, 165
Shrimp 98, 106, 107, 112
Snacks 35, 38, 85, 88, 90, 112, 115
Snow peas 100
Sodium 67, 69, 82
Sole 57
Soybean 79, 128, 132
Spinach 99, 100, 109-111
Stepfansson, Vilhyalmur 80
Stillman diet 28
Strawberries 98, 100, 103, 105, 108, 110, 112, 124
Stroke 67, 140
Sucrose 166
Sugar 24, 28, 38, 56, 61, 63, 65, 66, 68, 69, 76, 88, 98, 100, 103, 130,
              140, 156, 166
Supplements 17, 23, 89, 93, 96, 119, 121, 136-138,160,161
Swaps   87, 88, 90, 95-97, 102-104, 106-108, 110, 115-117, 150, 154
Sweet potatoes 126, 127
Swiss chard 99
Syrup 100

The Endocrine Control Diet   31
The Real Vitamin & Mineral Book   127
The Scarsdale Diet 28
Tofu 90, 102
Tomatoes 104, 106-108, 110, 111, 123, 126

Tossed salad 108, 109, 111
Trace minerals 131
Trans fatty acids 66, 154
Triglycerides 39, 47-51, 57, 58, 66, 86
Trout 93, 100, 133
Tuna 100, 112
Turkey 90, 98-100, 106-108, 110-112

Veal 100
Vitamin - A 126, 132
Vitamin - C 121, 124, 126, 129, 131, 136, 155, 165
Vitamin - E 126-128, 132, 136
V-8 juice 112

Walking 57, 157
Walnuts 93
Water 46, 50, 55, 72, 81-83, 89, 96, 100, 109, 111, 112, 132, 135,
          153,159,160
Water chestnuts 100
Wax beans 99
Weight control 139
Wine 28, 88, 98, 100, 109, 111, 112

Yogurt 90, 98, 99, 103-105, 112, 117, 155
Your Body Knows Best 40, 42
Yudkin, Dr. John 23, 24, 31, 166, 167

Zinc 131, 136
Zone Diet 73, 87, 90
Zone 10, 13, 15, 41-44, 69, 73, 85, 87, 90, 149-153, 165
Zone Perfect Meals in Minutes 42, 43, 85, 165
Zucchini 99, 109, 111

ABOUT THE AUTHOR

Dr. L. Lee Coyne is an exercise physiologist and nutrition consultant. He spent 16 years as a university professor, most recently at the University of Calgary, in Calgary, Alberta, Canada. A former fitness consultant to Canada's National Hockey Team, the National Alpine Ski Team and numerous other high caliber athletes. Lee currently works with selected Canadian Olympic Speedskaters and Canadian Olympic Biathletes. His son was a member of the Canadian Biathlon Team for 8 years and is now a full time coach. Most recently, he used his expertise as the nutrition coach for Mr. Jamie Clarke of Calgary, the successful leader of the 1997 Mount Everest Expedition. Lee conducted research and consulted in areas of exercise, sport, fitness and nutrition for employee health programs and for sport programs for many years. He left University teaching in 1981 to devote his time to nutrition and fitness lecturing, counseling, and writing throughout North America. He is President the Institute of Contemporary Nutrition and the author and designer of the self counseling "Sports Nutrition Coach" program currently used by many high performance athletes.

Lee is available for speaking engagements and seminars on **Sports Nutrition, Nutrition and Weight Management and Nutrition for the Diseases of the 90's**

For more information on Lee's seminars, video tapes and other educational materials you may contact Lee through Fish Creek Publishing at **1-800-668-4042** or **E-mail fish_creek@shaw.wave.ca**

ORDER FORM

✳   - Fax orders   (403) 225 - 2596

☎   - Telephone orders: Call Toll Free 1-(800) 668 - 4042

💻   - e-mail orders : fish_creek@shaw.wave.ca

      - web page www.ca.shaw.wave.ca/~leecoyne

✉   - Postal orders: **Fish Creek Publishing**
                240-70 - Shawville Blvd. S.W.#76084
                Calgary, AB, Canada, T2Y 2Z9.

Fat Won't Make You Fat - $13.95 U.S - $17.95 Canadian
Discounts for 10 -19 books = 10%, 20 or more   = 20%

Please send _____copie(s) of "Fat Won't Make You Fat" to:

Name:_____

Address: _____

City: _____State/Province_____

Zip/Postal Code_____ Telephone: (____)_____

E-mail address_____

Tax: include 7% for GST on all Canadian orders.
Shipping: include $4.00 for the first book and add $2.00
for each additional book
Payment: ☐ Cheque,   ☐ MasterCard,   ☐ Visa
          Card Number_____
Name on card:_____Exp.date____/___
       Call toll free, fax or E-mail and order now!!